STRATFORD
FOOD

STEVE STACEY

STRATFORD FOOD

An

EDIBLE HISTORY

Charleston   London

THE
History
PRESS

Published by The History Press
Charleston, SC 29403
www.historypress.net

Copyright © 2014 by Steve Stacey
All rights reserved

First published 2014

Manufactured in the United States

ISBN 978.1.62619.566.0

Library of Congress CIP data applied for.

This book is dedicated to my wife, Lisa:
a beautiful, food-loving person
from a beautiful, food-loving hometown.

Contents

Acknowledgements

There are many people and organizations that need to be thanked for their contribution to this book. First and foremost, the staff and management of the Stratford-Perth Archives bent over backwards to help me find historical food images from its vast annals. The photos they provided without charge are treasures, and this book would not be the same without them. Next, I would like to thank Savour Stratford and the Stratford Tourism Alliance for making the connection between The History Press and the author. When The History Press said it wanted to find a writer in Stratford who was interested in the food scene, Savour knew exactly who to call, and I really appreciate that. Thanks to the *Stratford Beacon Herald* for giving me access to some of its historic photos and to the Stratford Chefs School for providing some of the photos from its early years. Paul Finkelstein deserves a personal thank-you for providing me with some background on the food scene in Stratford before I lived here and, in general, for being a great friend and mentor to me. Danielle Brodhagen was the first person in the food community I met when I moved to Stratford, Ontario, and that fortuitous introduction set me off on a path that led me to write this book. I'd like to thank all the farmers who keep Stratford well fed with wonderful local products; without them, there would be no culinary stories to tell. I'd like to thank all the community members and staff at The Local Community Food Centre who are working together to make sure that everyone has access to the great food that makes Stratford such a special place to live. And finally, I would like to thank my family for being by my side on all of my adventures in food and, in particular, my wife, Lisa, for having such an incredible hometown!

Prologue

In her seminal study of global food cultures entitled *You Eat What You Are*, Canadian food historian Thelma Barer-Stein wrote of the link between the food that we eat and the cultures that we inhabit: "Food plays an inextricable role in our daily lives. Without food we cannot survive. But food is much more than a tool of survival. Food is a source of pleasure, comfort, and security. Food is also a symbol of hospitality, social status and religious significance. What we select to eat, how we prepare it, serve it, and even how we eat it are all factors profoundly touched by our individual cultural inheritance." Culture influences what we eat, and what we eat contributes to the development of a cultural identity.

In Stratford, following the history of food offers a unique window into the history and character of the city. Before the settlement of Stratford by Europeans, the only reason native peoples ever came to the site that would become the city was when they were hunting for food. The first permanent settlers were rugged pioneers who looked at a swamp and envisioned a farm and then set about to make that vision a reality by clearing land and planting crops. The heart of the city was focused around a market, and the downtown was built out from there, with the original market building also serving as the centre for all city business. When the railroads came, it was primarily to move food, as thousands and thousands of wagons full of wheat from the surrounding countryside were shipped to the urban centres.

When the wars began, the community showed its mettle and planted food gardens throughout the city in the name of victory. The appearance of the phenomenal Stratford Shakespeare Festival transformed the city into a centre for the arts, and countless eateries catering to theatregoers appeared—churches were changed into restaurants! When the increased demand for great food and talented people to cook it seemed impossible to meet, leaders stepped up to create a school to supply the culinary community with the country's best trained chefs. Alumni of the school went on to great culinary achievements of their own, including creating an innovative format for teaching young people about food by letting them cook for their peers. The city's responses to the problems of hunger and food insecurity reflects the trailblazing of the early pioneers, as groundbreaking programs work towards a vision of a place where people can sustain themselves with dignity and build community through the power of food. All of these things are celebrated once a year when the whole city is turned into a giant food carnival, recognized as the best culinary experience around!

The history of food in Stratford is the history of the city itself—a place where challenges are turned into opportunities, and the results put the community on the leading edge.

Chapter 1

Food Before It Was "Stratford"

The edible history of Stratford begins long before that name was given to the ten-square-mile area situated within the crosshairs of the Great Lakes of Lake Huron, Lake Ontario and Lake Erie. Before Stratford was ever settled permanently, it was still a place where prehistoric and First Nations people visited in search of food.

Starting about 2,500 years ago, the Late Paleolithic or Stone Age people, whose survival depended on subsisting through hunting and fishing, came to the forests and marshlands of the area to pursue game. Few artefacts from this era have been found in and around Stratford, suggesting that it was not of much interest, probably because it was not well drained and would have been quite swampy. However, farmers just outside Stratford today report that they occasionally come across an ancient stone spear or arrowhead in their fields, remnants of prehistoric hunting parties that might have been stalking the biggest of big game: woolly mammoth or mastodon. It has been noted that the prehistoric hunters of these megafauna—described by paleontologists as resembling an enormous cow—would have prized them as much for their huge tusks and shaggy coats as for their abundant meat.

For the indigenous First Nations communities in the region, there was a close relationship between the cultural patterns developed over thousands of years of inhabitation in the area and the natural world they depended on for their subsistence. Generally, regardless of whether it was the Hurons from around Sainte Marie, the Petuns to the west,

Neutrals from Lake Erie or the later Iroquois nations, the reason for their nomadic visits to the area that is now Stratford would have been for food. Specifically, they would come inland to hunt as part of an annual food sourcing routine: their permanent settlements would be inhabited in the summer; in the fall after the fishing season or harvest, the villages would then split up into smaller groups that would set out for winter hunting camps and then move into areas with maple trees for the maple sugar season in early spring. No permanent native settlements were set up in the area that is now Stratford; hunting parties would have come occasionally inland to hunt, but not with great frequency. In addition to bigger game such as deer (which also provided hides for shoes and clothing and bones and antlers for tools), these hunters would also pursue small game such as hare, partridge and geese. The mixed deciduous/coniferous forests found in the area would have provided berries and nuts as a nutritional supplement. The guiding principle was to develop a food store that could be drawn upon during times of scarcity.

In 1649, the Iroquois wiped out the villages of Sainte Marie, slaughtering the Hurons and their allies and burning their fields and shelters. This resulted in a blackout of any native activity in the area that would become Stratford for one hundred years, with no inland hunting parties coming through whatsoever. By the mid-eighteenth century, the Chippewas of the Ojibwa nation started settling around the region, and they, along with some Algonquin and Mississauga hunting parties, started coming to the Stratford area. But because the land around Stratford did not include navigable waterways, it was not attractive for native activity, so even hunting was something of a rarity.

In the era immediately preceding the European arrival and settlement of Stratford in the early to mid-nineteenth century, three distinct native communities would have included Stratford in their hunting territories: the Iroquois Six Nations, a mostly farming community from around the Grand River, looked to the land that included Stratford for their post-harvest hunts once their own traditional hunting lands were already appropriated under European colonization; the semi-nomadic Ojibwas; and the Oneidas, who had settled in the Lower Thames area south of Stratford to practice farming but accessed the territory around Stratford for hunting. For all three of these populations, the unsettled forest area that was to become the site of Stratford was a natural hunting ground that let them eke out their subsistence through trapping and hunting. But once settlement occurred, this way of life was completely threatened and ultimately rendered unsustainable.

In a historical example of tragic irony, the native peoples of the region were actually employed by the surveyors from the Canada Company—the British colonial group that would eventually purchase the lands of Perth and Huron Counties from the Chippewas and then systematically displace them—to help them survive in the less than hospitable terrain in and around what would soon become Stratford. For example, a team of surveyors that was establishing the Huron Road—the first thoroughfare in the area, one that would eventually link Guelph to Goderich via Stratford—found itself in a situation where its food supply was very scarce because horses couldn't get through to it. The group hired a Chippewa man who was living at the mouth of a river to fish for the surveying party; when the river froze, along with the Chippewa's remaining corn, a group of native and European hunters was assigned to go out and kill deer. The hunters survived until the horses could come: a fifteen-pound trout was caught, and venison they had hunted was dried to keep it from spoiling.

The Chippewa Ojibwas gave up the land that had been identified as the Huron Tract via Treaty 27½ on April 25, 1825. This opened the door for the Canada Company to sell land to the community that grew out of the surveyors' shanties on the banks of the river known as the Little Thames—the original site of Stratford. The salt beds on the south side of the Little Thames attracted deer and, in turn, native hunters; an encampment of Mississauga hunters would coat the ground with hair from deer they had harvested. Stratford's first group of European settlers would come across these native hunting camps, watching with keen interest as they butchered their freshly killed deer and trading goods for venison, bear meat, maple sugar and baskets.

However, this kind of mutually beneficial, reciprocal relationship did not endure. When the European settlers came and cleared the lands around Stratford for farming, it eradicated large amounts of habitat for deer and wild game, and the Chippewas were also threatened with trespassing charges when they travelled across farmlands that had previously been a source for game. The Europeans whittled away their hunting territories, and they were forced onto small reserves. They continued to sell and barter items like maple sugar and fish; however, they generally declined into conditions of poverty and were threatened with mass starvation, which was only held off by the annual annuities that came from the original Huron Tract land sales along with some government assistant programs.

Chapter 2

Stratford

Food City

On April 25, 1825, the British colonial land appropriation power known as the Canada Company acquired the Huron Tract—consisting of about 1 million acres in what included the future Perth and Huron Counties—from the Chippewa First Nation for the price of £145,150. In the area that surrounded what would eventually become Stratford, the company identified prime potential wheat-growing land—the land around Stratford was the Thames River plain, and because it was located south of a massive swamp, it was highly fertile with silts and nutrients. The abundant rainfall also made for good farmlands. The only challenge was that it all had to be cleared by hand.

The first settlers on the site of the Little Thames River that is now known as Stratford were surveyors who inhabited temporary riverside shanties. What they found was a stream with a "good mill seat" and a salt lick that attracted lots of deer. These first European visitors were cooking outdoors and washing in the river. This was known as "bush living"; it was recommended that the best gift that could be given to someone coming to settle in one of the shanties was a hunting dog for grouse. The first two white women to set foot on the land that is now Stratford were named Betsy Hill and Jane Good. They stopped by the river to cook lunch for their party using fires and cooking pots loaned by a work gang. Families had started to arrive to clear land for homesteads, making way for the first permanent settlement on that site.

The Shakespeare Hotel, the first permanent structure in Stratford (and site of the first vegetable garden). Operated by William Sargint and his family, the hotel burned down in 1849. *Stratford-Perth Archives.*

The first permanent structure in Stratford was created by William Sargint and his family: the Shakespeare Hotel. In the spring of 1832, Mrs. Sargint created Stratford's first garden, but she had to replant twice because of killing frosts. This clearly wasn't Ireland. No matter what a family's status, a garden with fruit trees, vegetables and shrubs was an important resource for everyday life to the settlers of Stratford in the 1830s.

Once the fields were ready to plant with crops, a gristmill for milling flour was created by the Canada Company alongside the existing sawmill in the winter of 1832. Both of these were purchased by an industrious gentleman named John Corry Wilson Daly, who also added a wool mill to attract farmers. His suite of mills was soon offering lumber, yarn, flour and oatmeal. Even in the midst of a rugged farming frontier, Daly and his family were concerned with maintaining an image of staunch propriety: they ate from the best china, and those who joined them for dinner were expected to adhere to rigid protocols; it was considered an insult to be seated "below the salt" at their family table and even worse to be told to go eat in the barn!

The riverside area that would soon become known as Stratford was developing into a centre for commerce. Back at the Shakespeare Hotel, the Sargints opened a store. Cooking pots were being created by blacksmiths and sold to settlers. A barter system was established, as produce from the newly cleared farms was exchanged for goods and services.

Irish, English, Scots and a few Welshmen were the majority of the new settlers and brought their customs to the emerging community; 30 percent of the settlers were of German origin. A pair of brothers named Seegmiller would often come over the Huron Road with a team of horses pulling a wagon loaded with flour, pork and whisky, which they were bringing to the port of Goderich to trade for salt, fish, hides and currency. In the 1860s, there was an overspill of Mennonites from the adjacent crowded Waterloo County. They were mainly farmers who kept to themselves, speaking their own language.

The Shakespeare Hotel burned down in 1849, marking the end of the era of early settlement. By 1852, there were nine hundred people living in the town that was now known as Stratford. Along with the gristmill, there were also mills dedicated to oats and barley. In 1854, the region in which Stratford was located became officially recognized as Perth County, and Stratford was incorporated as a village. By the 1850s, "muddy Stratford" had wooden sidewalks, with stores that fronted the streets. Heavy wagons full of wheat were rumbling from the nearby countryside to the Market Square. The retailers in town were mostly general stores, selling everything from whisky to bulk foods and long johns. Some stores in the 1850s had signs advertising "Country Produce Taken in Exchange," as there was still no banking system and bartering was a popular means of commerce.

Miss Katherine "Cowkitty" Bryden was a Scottish-born woman who operated the first commercial dairy in town. She lived with the cows, sharing the long building where they were raised. She loved her "beasties" and never married herself; the legend had it that she had planned to marry a missionary, but when that relationship failed, she never got over it.

A wheat crop failure in 1853, followed by the Crimean War, increased the worldwide demand for wheat and pushed the prices up to two dollars per bushel. This wheat boom brought prosperity to the Stratford area, with countless wagons per day coming to the Stratford

Interior of the Ballantyne Cheese Factory, circa 1895. Owned by the Honorable Thomas Ballantyne, who along with being a founder of the Canadian cheese industry also served as a politician whose career included tenure as Speaker of the House in Ontario parliament. *Stratford-Perth Archives.*

A winter Downie Street view, 1800s, with horse-drawn sleds. *Stratford-Perth Archives.*

Market Square from the farms nearby. New roads had to be created to accommodate the increased traffic from the countryside, and to pay for this new infrastructure, tollbooths were established. However, the spendthrift farmers soon figured out how to avoid the tolls by taking side roads.

Meanwhile, the railroad was making its way to Stratford, and upon its arrival, it would soon become established as Stratford's primary industry. The railroad and the farming industry would become closely interrelated; starting in 1856, thousands of wagons loaded with wheat came to Stratford to have their grain shipped out via the trains.

Plans were soon underway for a proper market building that would also serve as the town hall. By 1856, there were two main meat merchants, George Larkworthy and Christian Ubelacker, both of whom were looking forward to renting stalls in the pending new market building.

In 1860, a Board of Trade was established in Stratford, initially set up to assist farmers in their transactions. Its first function was to receive telegrams reporting on the grain markets in larger centres like Montreal and Buffalo and on updates on steamer ship traffic. The goal was to regulate the price of wheat so that area farmers could be assured that they were getting a fair price for their grain. Outside the village, however, farmers were skeptical, thinking that the board's true function was to keep the price of wheat down, and problems and conflicts arose.

In about 1866–67, there was widespread suspicion that dishonest dealings were common in Stratford, with rumours of fraud and deliberately inaccurate weighing of grain. These rumours became so prevalent that buyers from places like Buffalo refused to do commerce with the grain industry in Stratford unless the weights were guaranteed; the local trade committee therefore encouraged the city to install public weigh scales in the Market Square.

The Honorable Thomas Ballantyne, who was both a politician and a businessman, contributed a great deal to Canadian farmers; he built the Black Creek Cheese House in Downie Township in 1867 and was a founder of the cheese industry of Ontario. His political accomplishments included tenure as the Speaker of the House for the Ontario legislature.

By 1875, Stratford was developing business blocks. The Italian Warehouse was a grocery store that was located right alongside several other stores on the former Albion Hotel property.

By 1884, the population of Stratford was still well under ten thousand. It still had wooden sidewalks, and livestock regularly strolled along the unpaved city streets. In 1884, a bylaw was enacted banning farmers from letting their cows roam free in the city during certain times of year. The Corporation of the City of Stratford was inaugurated the next year in 1885, and it took on the title of the "Classic City." At that time, the first telephones were being installed in the more progressive and important addresses in town. This included cheesemaker Thomas Ballantyne.

The first telephone exchange was located at 47 Downie Street at a former fish market; the smell of fish from the former tenant was so strong in the floorboards that the stench had to be scrubbed out with carbolic acid.

In contrast to the depressed economic times of the 1880s, the turn of the century saw Stratford experiencing a boom: the roads were finally getting paved with asphalt, municipal water was being established and there were big construction projects underway, like the Queen's Hotel and the Grand Trunk Railway Building extension. Stratford found itself in an ideal strategic location between several large markets and was becoming a centre for manufacturing, in particular furniture, because of good access to shipping routes and good labour relations.

However, upon the arrival of World War I, the price for food in Stratford went through the roof. Eggs were twenty cents per dozen, and butter was thirty-five cents per pound, with milk at ten cents per quart. By 1916, there was a labour shortage on the area's farms; one hundred Stratford high school students were allowed to leave class early to work on farms alongside private citizens, soldiers on leave and workers on leave from their factory jobs.

By the 1930s, the previous reputation Stratford enjoyed as a place with favourable labour relations was disrupted. Labour movements were forming throughout North America, and the food sector in Stratford reflected this as its workers became organized and clashed with owners. At the Swift's Meat Packing Plant, there were mostly women working plucking chickens at two cents per bird. Even though these were mostly rural women who were terrified of losing their jobs in the unstable labour environment, they went on strike on September 21, 1933. The workers all walked out, trapping eleven thousand live chickens and four hundred ducks in the factory. The birds were allowed to be fed and then were taken under temporary seizure by the Humane Society. The strike was

Whyte Meat Packing Company delivery wagon, circa 1920s. *Stratford-Perth Archives.*

violent as sympathizers and strikers clashed with the police. The strikers released the chickens, and onlookers scrambled to collect them to take them home and eat; they also scooped up armloads of liberated butter from smashed trucks and railcars that were looted. After army tanks and machine guns were called in to keep the peace, the poultry dressers and their contemporaries at other factories in Stratford received a 10 percent raise and a workweek restricted to forty-four to fifty hours per week.

By the 1930s, downtown Stratford was a bustling centre for commerce, with four large department stores operating alongside specialist stores like Bradshaw's China Hall. The Whyte Meat Packing Company was a meat processor with a retail outlet at the corner of Downie and Wellington that was famous for its meats. Along the downtown streets of Stratford, people were met every morning with the aroma of fresh bread from the city's bakeries.

Other memorable food businesses deserve mention in this edible history of Stratford. A well-known German delicatessen was the

Interior, Whyte Meat Packing Company processing floor and butcher staff. *Stratford-Perth Archives.*

Stratford Packers, where people could get meat, cheeses, breads and pickles. Today, that business is called the Butcher and the Baker and continues to be a favourite destination for those seeking out deli products and baked goods.

Corner grocery stores and small markets such as Puddicombe Farms Market were the main channels for food shopping before the appearance of supermarkets. In 1928, the store run by William Wolfe on the corner of Cambria and Nelson Streets was typical of the neighbourhood variety

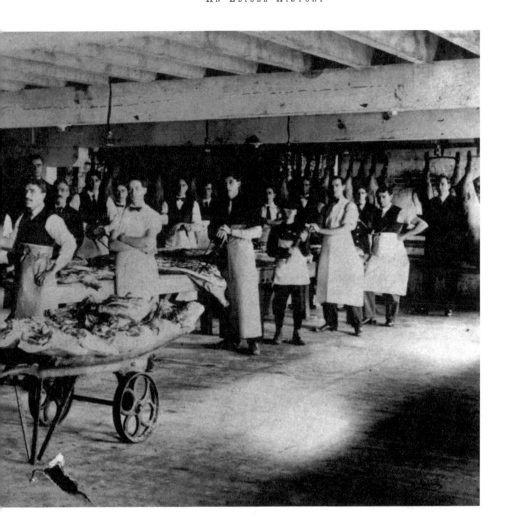

stores that were found throughout the city. Allens Fruit Market—on Wellington Street right beside what is now named Allens Alley—was particularly neat and attractive inside, with coloured tiles and fruit-shaped lights. Barnsdale's Trading Company, located at 27–31 Market Place, was one of the largest stores in the city and sold groceries but also everything else, including hardware and prescriptions. It was especially well known for its baked goods and puff pastries. Early in the twentieth century, Lloyd's Wholesale Produce would have supplied many of the

Puddicombe Farms Market, a typical example of the small street market most people in Stratford largely depended on for food shopping. *Stratford-Perth Archives.*

grocers in town with its seven delivery trucks. W.J. McCully's was one of the largest independent grocery stores in the province around the 1920s and provided a particularly impressive selection of fruits and vegetables. Upon arrival, patrons would sit on stools and tell the clerk what they wanted; an employee would then fetch their items. If a person ordered butter, they would bring a sample on a toothpick so the customer would know it was fresh.

Fish and chips have always been a popular meal for Stratford families and visitors. Ruby Stewart's Fish and Chips restaurant on Downie Street was popular during the 1930s. The Viking was famous as the best fish and chips place in town for many years, but more recently, the short-lived Simple Fish and Chips was the talk of the town with its all sustainable fish and seafood menu.

Bakeries included Blue Boy and Dorothy's Bakery, while today, the Downie Street Bakehouse is known to have the finest fresh-baked breads in town. Fanfare Books used to have a café in it featuring local bread, cheese, ham and cider, a fact that would probably surprise most current residents of Stratford.

The Cheese House, on Erie Street, had cheese that was ripened and aged, and it served as headquarters of the Perth Headwater

Interior of Allens Fruit Market, known for its neatness and cleanliness. It is the namesake of today's Allens Alley. *Stratford-Perth Archives.*

Delivery van for Lloyd's Wholesale Produce delivery service—one of seven delivery trucks in the fleet. *Stratford-Perth Archives.*

Cheese Company; today, Monforte Dairy is one of the premier artisan cheesemakers in Ontario, and a new Monforte osteria-style restaurant on Wellington Street features its sheep and goats milk cheese in different dishes every day.

Bradshaw's has long been known as the place to get fine china, which it imported wholesale, as well as other dinner accompaniments. Today, Bradshaw's continues to provide the Stratford community with opportunities to purchase wonderful products for the kitchen.

Olin Brown was a well-known confectioner. He sold his business, and at the same time the ownership changed, one of his former employees, Rheo Thompson, set up shop at 26 Brunswick Street, where people were able to get a peek at the chocolate makers in action. Today, Rheo Thompson Candies is under new ownership, but it continues to be renowned for its signature mint smoothies, which have over time become synonymous with the city itself—any Stratford resident visiting someone outside the city is expected to always bring along a box of these mint chocolate treats. A second confectioner, Derek Barr of Chocolate Barr's, has recently moved to a new location in the former site of the Sun Room restaurant on George Street; there he will continue to have fun making products like giant Easter bunnies and jumbo candy canes while also creating fine chocolate truffles that might even rival the Rheo mint smoothie in quality and taste. From 1870 to 1960, Rankins was known as the place to go for refreshments from the soda fountain, ice cream treats and toasted sandwiches, but it was also known for its hand-rolled chocolates.

One family-run store that continues to sell food to the Stratford community is the Gentle Rain on Rebecca Street. Eric and Marsha Eberhardt founded the store in 1979 and moved to their new location on Rebecca Street in 1989. The business has grown quickly over the years, selling health food products and local and sustainable food in many forms. The current store has solar panels on the roof and employs no fewer than two dozen retail staff. Sadly, in July 2010, Eric Eberhardt passed away; he will be remembered as a leader and visionary in the Stratford food community.

Established in 2011, Your Local Market Co-op is a retail grocery store with a takeout counter and an on-site bakery. The founding members of the cooperative started the business to provide steady, year-round employment for those who were committed to working in the culinary industry. Sourcing virtually all of its products from Ontario, this Downie

Street oasis brought food retailing back to the downtown core of the city. Stratford local food lovers have since delighted in the opportunity to get great local produce on weekdays, when the farmers' markets are not open. Artisan baked goods and value-added products line its shelves, and its takeout counter is a popular lunch spot, with quality food made daily from scratch and offered at a great price. In 2013, the workers cooperative launched a second site, the Slave to the Grind coffee shop on Ontario Street, and in 2014, there are plans for a takeout window behind the café on York Street.

Chapter 3

Farmers

Producing the Bounty

The evolution of Perth County from an unwanted swamp to a county with some of the highest values and revenues for farmland/ farming in Ontario was achieved by the people. First the pioneers had to clear the whole county, which was covered with mixed deciduous/ coniferous forest, by hand. Every acre of farmland was created by chopping down trees and pulling out stumps and roots. Then they had to create roads to get the farm production to markets. The next step was to create a railroad to get it to the even bigger markets. In 1863, Perth County produced more than 1 million bushels of wheat, and the railroad was able to carry this to the broader market to the profit of the farming community.

Twenty years after the Huron Road was established, the area's farms were generating a surplus of farm productivity that could be exported. At first, families had barely been able to produce enough for themselves. After 1845, the forest clearings spread quickly, and the increase in farmland translated into higher production levels of wheat and other grains, as well as pork and butter. There was a market for food in the areas east of Stratford, and the farmers of the area wanted to tap into it. Therefore, they were in support of enhanced transportation such as roads and railroads.

The County of Perth invested a great deal into making the area around Stratford favourable for agriculture. Public funds were used to create drainage schemes to allow for the wetland to become profitable for farmers. At one time, it was suggested that areas of Perth County had the greatest concentration of tile drains on the entire continent.

At that time, Stratford was located at the corners of Ellice, North and South Easthope and Downie Townships. In these four townships in 1849, there was a total population of 7,244 farm residents, cultivating 27,398 acres of farmland. In 1850, these farms produced 118,000 bushels of wheat, 2,000 bushels of barley, 98,000 bushels of oats, 14,000 bushels of peas, 56,000 bushels of potatoes, 43,000 bushels of turnips, 76,000 pounds of maple sugar, 19,600 pounds of butter and 15,900 pounds of wool.

The first blacksmith in Stratford, John Sharman, began by hammering out shoes for oxen and horses, but he expanded to become a family foundry, ultimately manufacturing farm implements and machinery. On a farm on the outskirts of Stratford, John Sharman's son, an emerging industrialist named Joseph, became interested in a breed of cattle just beginning to get attention in Ontario—the white-faced Herefords of England. The first of this cattle breed were imported to Guelph in 1861 and had done well. Joseph sent his own son, Harry, who had just graduated from the Agricultural College at Guelph, to England to select breeding stock. Not long after registering its first two bulls ("President Grant" and "Tom Wilton") in 1885, Sharman and Son became recognized as a forerunner in the Hereford breeding industry in Canada. Upon their moving on, the Sharman Farm became part of the Stratford Agricultural Grounds.

Way back in 1841, John Linton—a straight-laced Presbyterian who was also very committed to his new rural community—called for the creation of an agricultural society. The Stratford (Branch) Agricultural Society was established. The newly created ag society used the Shakespeare Hotel as its headquarters and planned the first exhibition in October 1841 around that property and its adjacent streets, which became known as Shakespeare Place.

Pens were constructed to accommodate pigs, sheep, oxen and cattle. The prize money was a total of twenty pounds, five shillings (less than forty-five Canadian dollars today). Prize categories included best yoke of oxen (at least five years old); ten yards of homemade cloth (any colour), best wool grown and spun by the exhibitor; best woolen mittens; best hooked matts; finest twenty-five-pound block of butter; and prizes for the best homemade farm implements. The best bull and the best stallion netted their owners the top prize money, which was one pound.

John J.E. Linton settled in Stratford in 1833 and, along with other accomplishments, initiated the Stratford Agricultural Society in 1841. *Stratford-Perth Archives.*

In 1844, it added field crop competitions; in 1846, the Agricultural Society held its first Ploughing Match; in 1846, it added the first Standing Root competition; and in 1855, it had the first of what was supposed to become a monthly Fat Cattle Show (it only lasted one year).

In 1857, the Stratford (Branch) Agricultural Society paid the Canada Company £200 for an acre of land to create a permanent fairground. This was initially moved from Shakespeare Place to the property of Stratford's first schoolhouse, located where the public library is today. In 1859, the fair organizers signed a ten-year lease on land between Downie Street, St. Patrick Street and George Street (where the police station is today) for rent equal to the tax levy. In 1860, for the first time, the fair charged admission to help support the increasing costs of the event. In 1865, the fair grew to a two-day event, and it continued to move around; it was moved to the countryside location of O'Loane and Huron Streets and then slightly closer to town at Forman and Huron. By 1868, it still didn't have a permanent fairgrounds. In 1876, the agricultural society finally traded the property at the west end of Britannia Street for twenty acres, and after clearing the brush-covered property, it built a permanent fairground building called the Crystal Palace and a racetrack. However, it sold that and continued to move around. Then, in 1911, it bought the Britannia Street site back. In 1965, a new building called the Coliseum was built on that property to host the Fall Fair, as well as other community events. By this time, the Fall Fair also included a cooking school, and meals were being served by St. Andrews Church out of the old curling lounge. Different churches took over the lounge to serve food each year.

Even through the tough times of the 1930s, Stratford celebrated the farming community that surrounded and fed it. In 1930, the city hosted its first International Ploughing Match, and in 1936, twenty-five thousand people came through the gates of the Fall Fair.

Farming around Stratford was also a contributor to the war effort. During the Second World War, in the 1940s, the farmers of the area were encouraged to do soil tests and determine exactly how much fertilizer they needed to maximize crops. While many Fall Fairs were cancelled during the war, in Stratford they continued, sponsoring field crop competitions to facilitate enhanced production of wheat, barley and corn.

In 1974, the Ontario Pork Congress was held for the first time in Stratford. At that time, Perth marketed more hogs than any other county in Ontario. In 1988, there were 1,544 registered hog producers in the county, producing 656,057 pigs for a total of $73,104,000. The Pork Congress is a three-day event that attracts more than ten thousand people and is known among pork producers as the finest event of its kind anywhere in North America. Today, it takes place on the agricultural society's fairgrounds/Agriplex. As an example of a unique relationship that probably could only happen in Stratford, the annual Blues Festival has joined forces with the Pork Congress to include an impressive rib barbecue contest each June—Perth County pork ribs are slow-cooked by experts and judged by community members who aren't afraid to be seen in public with barbecue sauce on their faces!

Certainly, the experience of farming in the Stratford area has changed over time. One historical testimony by a local farmer narrated the transition that took place in the farms that surrounded and fed Stratford throughout the late twentieth century. While growing up in the 1930s, the farmer worked with his father and uncles and recalled the new Fordson tractor they got in 1937. At thirteen, he was taken out of school to work full time with his father on the farm. When he was sixteen, his father formed a partnership with him. He took over the farm completely in 1968. After buying that first tractor, the farmers still used horses occasionally—for example, for pulling wagons that straw was forked onto during threshing. A second tractor saw most of the work that had been performed by the horses eradicated. A lot of work still had been done by hand, such as feeding animals and mucking out stalls. During the 1940s, farming was very lucrative as prices continually stayed high. Farms were much smaller than they are today: twelve to twenty cows was considered a good-sized milking herd. The farm families milked by hand and poured fresh milk into a separator, with the skim milk going to the pigs and the cream going into Stratford to the creamery on Erie Street. They also kept chickens and graded and candled the eggs that they would deliver to households in Stratford every week.

Then things changed further as the industrialization of agriculture progressed. The quota system was set up, and mechanical milkers were introduced. But to increase supply to meet quota or to upgrade to mechanical milkers would have been a big expense, so the farmer switched to beef cattle and kept a small crop of chickens for farmgate sales. Quotas and the growing automation of farming resulted in farms becoming highly specialized rather than the mixed family farms of the past. Certainly many of these specialized, automated farms have been highly successful financially, as farmers in Perth County are some of the most economically successful in the entire province.

However, there are still many mixed family farms around Stratford that today supply the restaurant industry, some stores in the retail community like the Gentle Rain and Your Local Market Co-op and households through Community Supported Agriculture (CSA) programs. Most of these farms also participate in farmers' markets in Stratford or as far away as Waterloo or London, Ontario.

Ryan Bergman and Mindy Griffiths started their organic vegetable farming operation, Loco Fields, on rented land outside of Amulree back in 2011. Today, their farm is outside of Sebringville and includes heritage and heirloom varieties of greens, tomatoes and other veggies, as well as unique products such as organic local ginger. They have recently begun distributing local meat and other products produced on neighbouring farms to their customers.

Warren Ham of August's Harvest farm near Gadshill is one of the most prolific growers of organic garlic in North America. He has developed a line of value-added garlic and Saskatoon berry items, and his products are shipped all over the continent. He is also one of the founders of the popular Stratford Garlic Festival ("The Festival that Really Stinks"), which has been taking place annually since 2007.

If Perth County is most well known as "Pork Country," then Fred and Ingrid DeMartines of Perth Pork Products might be its most celebrated ambassadors. They have been raising pigs on their farm outside Sebringville since moving there from Holland in 1979, but in the 1990s, they began to switch from raising nothing but commodity pork in pens to pasture-raising heritage breeds including Tamworth (aka the "bacon pig") and Berkshire. But perhaps most impressively, since 1992 their farm has been home to a rowdy herd of wild boar, and their products include wild boar bacon and wild boar sausages. Many visitors to the farm have been invited to scoop a few shovels full of walnuts collected from neighbours' trees for the wild boar to crunch on. Perth Pork Products gained widespread attention for its wild boar operation when it was visited by Chef Lynne Crawford for her Food Network Canada show *Pitchin' In*, which saw her mucking out boar poop before heading to the kitchen to create a wonderful meal using this unique local meat. For years, the best chefs and butcher shops in Toronto, including Jamie Kennedy and the Healthy Butcher, have been receiving heritage pork and wild boar hand-delivered by Fred himself during his weekly delivery run.

Within walking distance from Perth Pork Products is another famous local producer, Soiled Reputation Farm. Run by Welshman Antony John and his wife, Tina Vanden Heuvel, for more than thirty years, Soiled Reputation greens and other products are featured on the menu of virtually every good restaurant in Stratford, as well as many in Toronto. The small-scale, intensive organic vegetable operation and its offbeat operators were the subject of the 2003–4 Food Network Canada classic *The Manic Organic*, which was also shown on Home and Garden TV and broadcast in fifty countries.

Also just outside Sebringville is the mixed family farm known as Erbcroft Farm. Luann and Tim Erb raise everything from ducks to goats, chickens and llama, but they are best known for their lamb products. Chefs in Stratford swear by Erbcroft lamb, which is available at their farmgate or at the Stratford Farmers' Market every Saturday.

The list of farmers who are putting in the extra work to provide high-quality food for local consumers is long. Church Hill Farm outside Punkeydoodle Corners pasture raises English Black Pigs, and this product is featured on the menus of most of the best restaurants in Stratford. Shallot Hill Farm produces (predictably) many bushels of shallots each season, as well as garlic and other products like heirloom carrots. Pork from Lassdale Farm is a favourite of restaurateur Craig Foster of Foster's Inn, who has regularly partnered with farmer Mark Lass for the Savour Stratford Culinary Festival's Tasting Tent. Other local farms include producers of water buffalo, elk, trout, pheasant, quail, emu, goat and grass-fed beef. Basically, if there is a farm-fresh product that a resident or chef in Stratford would like to find, there is in all likelihood a local producer who can supply it.

Chapter 4

Markets

The Original Heart of the City

In 1855, a former Canada Company surveyor named Donald McDonald sold the village of Stratford one triangular acre of land between Wellington, Downie and George Streets. The price—a mere £200—was a steal for the city. But the deed came with a very specific condition: the village was "to have and to hold the said land and premises and appurtenances…in trust to use the same for the purpose of erecting and maintaining a Market House and the buildings incident thereto as aforesaid forever."

McDonald was not himself a market vendor, nor did he make this stipulation to ensure that food remained a central part of the social fabric of Stratford, bringing people together each week in the central public space that became officially known as Market Square. Rather, he was a shrewd landowner who observed that with the coming of the railroad, there might be a migration of businesses south towards the train station. His land was all downtown, and he wanted to keep downtown as the focal point for Stratford social and commercial activities to enhance the value of his land.

In 1857, the original Market Building was erected. In 1856, the town fathers took the money they had been paid back after loaning it to create the railway through Stratford and put it towards the construction of an enormous building. Although it was named the Market Building, the white brick edifice with stone facings had another covert purpose: to serve as a town hall, with half used for government purposes and the other half for market purposes.

The original Market Building, erected in 1857, also served as town hall. *Stratford-Perth Archives.*

Opposite: In the Market Building, the lower floor was divided into stores that were used as butcher shops, while the upper floors housed city government. *Stratford-Perth Archives.*

In terms of its market features, the building design included four stores flanking the main entrance, butcher stalls facing south back into the square, a market house, public weigh scales and a busy little grocery store owned by one Mrs. Patterson. In between was an open space where farmers could bring their produce to sell in the square. As far as its town hall features, the Market Building also included a fire hall, police quarters, jail cells, a concert hall, council chambers and government offices.

The stores and the butcher stalls were auctioned off for rental, and the bidding for the stores began at $120 per year, while the butcher stalls went for $32. As far as the costs the city had to bear to accommodate this market, it hired a caretaker at $7 a month in the winter and $4 a month in the summer. It also hired a market clerk to administer the market who was paid the (then exorbitant) salary of $24 dollars per month.

The first non-government occupants of the Market Building were John McCrea, who ran a flour and feed store and who also sold fresh fish from Lake Huron, and W.M. Clarke, who ran a dry goods and grocery business. Other tenants were listed as "merchants" or "tradesmen."

Even though they had secured themselves a prime location in the new downtown market, the butchers immediately began to complain. There were no toilet facilities for them to use, nor was there any heat to keep them warm. In response, the city spent forty dollars to construct an outdoor privy on Market Square, and two wood stoves were installed in the Market Building. Then it was the city councillors' turn to complain about the butchers: they were told they could not drag their carcasses through the front hall of the building because it stunk up the upstairs city hall chambers.

The shared location of a market and a city hall certainly came with unique challenges and created strange bedfellows. But the "McDonald

Market Place on market day. *Stratford-Perth Archives.*

Opposite, top: Rebuilding the burned-down site of the Market Building into a city hall completely devoid of the market features stipulated on the deed to the property. *Stratford-Perth Archives.*

Opposite, bottom: Market Place, Wellington Street, with market tables. New City Hall is at top left. *Stratford-Perth Archives.*

Proviso" on the deed to the land was being met, and the need to have a city building was being accomplished alongside the market...at least for the time being.

The area was further developed with a public market space in mind. The vacant space at the rear of Market Square was graded, and a platform and sheds were installed to provide shelter to patrons and vendors. Then, in 1887, Donald McDonald's widow sold the city another strip of land between Wellington and Downie Streets for the princely sum of one dollar, again on the agreement that it would only be used for a market space and on a second condition that the city replace a broken wooden sidewalk with pavement and tear down a rickety old wooden railing.

The terms to maintain the property with a Market Square and a Market Building were being followed, with additional functions of housing city government snuck in, when disaster struck. Early in the morning on November 24, 1897, a police constable spotted a red glow emanating from the windows of the Market Building. Unfortunately, the fire department had moved to a new location a few years earlier, and the limited volunteer firefighters available were unable to quell the raging inferno as the Market Building/town hall went up in flames. Everyone watched on as the blaze grew completely out of hand. The market tenants—the butchers and the feed merchants—could only look on helplessly as their stock and equipment burned to the ground.

Somehow, when the city started formulating plans to rebuild, there was no hint of a market anywhere in the designs. The McDonald Proviso was ignored as a new red brick city hall was created without a single market feature. However, although there were no butcher shops or stores anymore, the Market Square was still used for an outdoor farmers' market and remained a bustling place where citizens could meet. So the McDonald stipulation was still being maintained, however loosely since the primary function of the property was now clearly city business.

At around the turn of the century, the newly formed Board of Parks Management proposed that the Market Square be severed off from the city hall and turned into a greenspace with gardens, benches and grass. This was rejected, and the original conditions of sale were cited as the reason why the city couldn't change a market space into a park.

Then, just a few years later, the market was moved to a city-owned building behind the fire hall on Waterloo Street, and Market Square was turned into a parking lot.

When the city received a proposal that it build a "Comfort Station" (otherwise known as a public toilet) in Market Square in 1925, the city clerk looked into its legality and soon determined that virtually none of the features on this historic property conformed with the mandated stipulations of the original sale. The presence of the city hall and the absence of anything resembling a farmers' market were breaches of trust, and therefore "any ratepayer in the City might bring forward an action to enforce the terms of this conveyance."

Opposite, top: Market Place on market day, teeming with patrons and farmers' wagons. *Stratford-Perth Archives.*

Opposite, bottom: Stratford Farmers' Market, relocated behind the Waterloo Street fire hall. *Stratford-Perth Archives.*

Stratford Farmers' Market, relocated to the fairgrounds, circa 1972. *Stratford-Perth Archives.*

In 1967, Canada's centennial year, the farmers' market vendors once again found themselves displaced as the city sold their building behind the fire station to the Woolworth's chain to set up a store. The market moved once again, this time to the fairgrounds, where it rented space from the Stratford Agricultural Society. Vendor fees had to be increased, and the space itself was insufficient, as twenty-five vendors attempted to squeeze into a poultry barn that was just twenty feet by one hundred feet. The vendors who remembered the McDonald Proviso were resentful towards the city for forcing them to rent space outside of the downtown—the city had clearly reneged on the deal it had agreed to once in 1855 and then again in 1887.

The market vendors dropped to ten around frustrations over the vendors fees and the unfavourable conditions. But those who remained stuck it out, with some community support, until a 6,500-square-foot annex was added on to the poultry shed in 1970; this saw the market rebound. Then, in 1984, the poultry building was replaced altogether with a more modern market facility created by the agricultural society. This soon resulted in the regular participation of fifty vendors weekly, with sixty vendors in the peak months.

Having operated continuously since 1855, the Stratford Farmers' Market can claim to be one of the oldest markets in Ontario, and it continues to operate every Saturday year-round at the Stratford Agriplex. Vendors today include elk farmers, egg sellers, local meat purveyors, cheese mongers, bakers, soup makers and producers of virtually every vegetable under the sun, including seasonal vendors of corn, strawberries and asparagus.

However, there is a second farmers' market that has more recently sprung up in Stratford: the Slow Food Sunday Market. Slow Food is an international movement that was started in Italy in 1986 by an activist named Carlos Petrini. Launched as an organization that would counter the dominant force of industrialized fast-food chains, Slow Food champions local family farms, culturally significant and traditional ingredients, sustainable environmental practices in the production of food and artisanal small businesses. In a world where globalization, standardization, industrialization and genetic modification are coming to more and more characterize the food that people eat, Slow Food encourages everyone to slow down and take the extra time necessary to cook from scratch, grow organic gardens, enjoy the company of others around the dinner table and celebrate each region's unique food heritage.

Slow Food Perth County is the local chapter (or "convivium") promoting "Good, Clean and Fair" food in Stratford and the mostly rural community that surrounds it. Established more than a decade ago, the group has consistently participated in events and initiatives to educate and advocate around local food produced in ethical and sustainable ways.

However, in June 2010, the members of Slow Food Perth County took its work to another level, taking the courageous step to actively change the food system in Stratford towards a more sustainable model. It launched the Slow Food Sunday Market.

That summer, Monforte Dairy cheesemaker Ruth Klahsen invited Slow Food Perth County to run a market in the back lot of her brand-new dairy on Griffith Road. With a handful of vendors who reflected the values of the Slow Food organization—including Soiled Reputation organic farm, Anything Grows gardening boutique, Creton's Garden Fresh Produce & Herbs and Koert Organics—the new market started off slow, appropriately enough. But as the season progressed, more and

Tim Creton from Creton's Garden Fresh Produce & Herbs is a fixture at both the Stratford Farmers' Market and the Slow Food Sunday Market. *Stratford Tourism Alliance.*

more people started making the trip to the edge of town to see what the buzz was about for this new market that was connecting the community to some of the best food available in Ontario.

When the outdoor market season ended in October, Slow Food was invited to set up an indoor market in the vaulted ceilinged basement of the Anything Grows garden store (located in a historic building that was once a brewery). As the winter months passed, the Slow Food vendors proved that Stratford could go local and sustainable in its food choices throughout the year.

That winter, the coordinators of the market were approached by the Stratford City Centre Committee. What the committee proposed was nothing short of remarkable: the Slow Food Market should relocate to downtown Market Square in the summer of 2011! No market had operated there in more than one hundred years. The passionate activists and committed vendors knew that this was a once in a lifetime opportunity and didn't hesitate to take the City Centre Committee up on its offer. Council (perhaps aware of the long-neglected McDonald Proviso) approved a road closure on Market Square every Sunday from June to

October. And with a fanfare from the Stratford Police Pipe and Drum Band, the Slow Food Sunday Market launched its downtown operations on June 5, 2011. A farmers' market was finally back in Market Square.

Since then, the Slow Food Sunday Market has continued indoors during the winter in different locations, including the old Kalbfleish Motors showroom (alongside the new site of the Stratford Brewing Company) and, most recently, The Local Community Food Centre. But it is definitely the outdoor summer market that the community has embraced as both a place to get fantastic local and sustainably produced food and a public space to socialize, listen to music and come together in the centre of town. Parallel events have partnered with the market, including the annual Slow Food Pork Party, where volunteers actually slow-roast a pig on a spit in Market Square overnight to serve to the community the next day, and Food Truck Eats, where some of the best food trucks in Ontario set up alongside the market to serve throngs of hungry people amazing street food.

Today, the slow progress of the market has steadily evolved into a thriving centre of community activity. Thirty vendors will participate in the 2014 season, including spectacular heritage veggies from Loco Fields, grass-fed meats by McIntosh Farm, sprouts by Kawthoolei Farm, and even a Slow Food Youth booth where young people who are interested in "Good, Clean and Fair" food provide snacks and information while fundraising to create food gardens in African schools through Slow Food International's 10,000 Gardens in Africa Campaign.

As the City of Stratford entertains plans for finally converting Market Square into a greenspace, it would be well advised to recognize the Slow Food Market as a fulfillment of the McDonald Proviso. A suitable design for the new Market Square would include resources for accommodating market vendors and patrons on Sundays. And if the new design prohibits a market, it might be time for a "ratepayer in the City" to "bring forward an action to enforce the terms of this conveyance."

Chapter 5

Where to Eat in Stratford

Stratford today is well known as an Ontario restaurant hotspot, largely due to the influx of diners travelling to the city in the spring, summer and fall to attend the Stratford Shakespeare Festival. However, what is less well known is that food service was one of the earliest commercial endeavors during the initial period of settlement along the Huron Road and continued to be important through the subsequent periods of the farming and railway booms.

When Stratford was still being surveyed by those who were trailblazing the Huron Road, which would eventually connect Guelph to Goderich, there was a complete lack of hospitality along the route: nowhere to get a hot dinner, nowhere to sleep and nowhere to get a drink. The Huron Road didn't have a single inn or tavern until John Galt proposed that "Houses of Entertainment" would be established every twenty miles. He knew that he'd need to provide subsidies to attract innkeepers to the wild country, so he offered forty pounds for men who would be willing to provide rudimentary hospitality. The earliest innkeepers didn't have to pay the Canada Company for land to settle—the Canada Company paid them!

The comfort station created nearest to Stratford was established by Sebastian Fryfogel, and the construction of what would become the Fryfogel Inn was underway by December 1828. The historic Fryfogel Inn building still stands today not far to the east of the hamlet of Shakespeare, about ten miles from Stratford. Reports indicate that the

The Fryfogel Inn was established by Sebastian Fryfogel in the late 1820s. Subsidies were provided to create places for food and lodging along the Huron Road during early settlement. *Stratford-Perth Archives.*

hospitality at the Fryfogel Inn was warm, but the fare was primitive and questionable—cucumbers pickled in whisky, greasy steaks and peas served in a washbasin.

Another nearby hostelry or "centre house" to the west of Stratford on the Huron Road was established by Andrew Seebach. A Canada Company employee stopped in hoping for a simple meal of fried pork, bread and butter with tea. Instead, he was given "Indian meal bread," a large cake of beef tallow fat and crust coffee with no milk or sugar. It was explained that the innkeeper was away fifty miles to go to the mill and a store to get flour, groceries and other ingredients.

In Stratford itself, by 1856, there were eleven hotels, a brewery and distillery; by 1871, there were twenty-five hotels and taverns, four saloons and five liquor shops. Before the century was over, it's been proposed that thirty-eight hotels were in existence at one time. Keeping track of all of the hotels and taverns that have operated in Stratford in the 1800s has

The Cabinet Hotel stood on Wellington Street's Easson Block. At one time, there were an estimated thirty-eight hotels in Stratford, mostly accommodating farmers who travelled into town to sell grain to be shipped via the newly established railroads. *Stratford-Perth Archives.*

proven difficult, with names and owners changing all the time, but the list has been described as "awesome."

Places with names like the Market Hotel, the New Found Out, the Palmerston, the Mansion House and the Royal Shipman were not just places to sleep; they were also places to eat. The Terrapin Hotel was said to have the best food in town; Pethick's Hotel near the train station advertised "Express trains stop long enough for passengers to take refreshments." The hundreds of farmers who hauled their wagons into Stratford were prevalent hotel patrons and had a lot to do with the creation of all these hotel establishments.

Saloons were also places where people could get both a drink and something to eat. The most popular was Ben Sleets Market Refreshment

The original wood and timber Queen's Arms at 161 Ontario Street. *Stratford-Perth Archives.*

The rebuilt Queen's Inn remains an Ontario Street landmark and continues to provide accommodation, as well as food and drink at the popular Boars Head Pub. *Stratford-Perth Archives.*

Hall, where it was advertised a hungry tippler could get "oysters, fried and pickled pigs feet, tripe and other refreshments." Assumedly, these were better when washed down with a beer or whisky.

Of the many hotels that existed in the 1800s, several still exist in one form or another today. The Dominion House (established in 1870) is still a popular watering hole situated near the train station, and the Queen's Inn (rebuilt in 1906 from the Queen's Arms) is an Ontario Street landmark that now also includes the Boars Head Pub. The Olde English Parlour still sits at the corner of St. Patrick and Wellington Streets and was originally called the Mansion House Hotel when it was established in the 1870s. Dignitaries travelling along the Grand Trunk Railway were put up there when stopping through Stratford.

However, without a doubt it was the inception of the Stratford Shakespeare Festival in 1953 that influenced the development of the city as a culinary destination with opportunities for fine dining, more relaxed bistros and restaurants to suit virtually every taste and palate. The Stratford Festival brought diners in droves; indeed, at first it was difficult for the local hospitality industry to keep up with the demand, but eventually a cast of local restaurateurs was able to stage nightly culinary performances that lived up to the superlative theatrics taking place in the Festival, Avon and Tom Patterson Theatres.

The small city of Stratford, nestled in a region that was mostly known for agriculture, was initially considered an unlikely place to see some of the world's finest actors. One newspaper reviewer wrote as he travelled to the first festival performance (*Richard III*) in 1953, "When I get to the end of all these wheat fields I'm not going to see Alec Guinness…it will have to be some other Guinness—Joe Guinness or somebody."

In 1957, the young Canadian actor Christopher Plummer came to play the role of Hamlet. He moved into the Queen's Inn for what was supposed to be temporary accommodation but could not be budged. The hotel proprietors eventually let him stay in their own suite and moved into the furnished house that the festival had booked for him to use for the season.

The emergence of the theatre had a ripple effect across the whole city. "In a community where Saturday night at the movies had been a lively weekend for many young people, now Tom Patterson could turn up at the Edinburgh Lounge at the Queen's Hotel with Ethel Merman. And once Edward Everett Horton had to stand at the bar because he didn't have a reservation for a table."

The festival changed Stratford economically and culturally. One newspaper reporter writing about the transformation indicated that Stratford had been a "meat and potatoes town" before the festival arrived. In fact, the early festival seasons saw more people coming to visit than the city could feed or accommodate. Private homes were opened to visitors who could not find local accommodation, and in the first year, there were local church dinners created to meet the increased demand for food that the strained restaurants could not supply. When the festival was first launched, a train that was sponsored by the *Toronto Telegram* newspaper brought theatregoers to the train station in Stratford, where they boarded a bus to take them to either Parkview United Church or Knox Presbyterian Church for a lunch that was served by their respective women's groups. After the show, they would get right back on the train and go home. There were not enough restaurants or places to stay to accommodate them all—they could only have been billeted at a private home or could stay at the YMCA.

New money from the theatre patrons was recognized as having a positive effect on the Stratford economy. New restaurants materialized to cater to the before- and after-theatre crowds, including the old, deconsecrated Congressional Church. One of the old grocery stores that had been a fixture for local residents' food sources was changed into a high-end gourmet and crystal shop selling imported coffee and snails. In 1966–67, a survey was conducted of visiting theatre patrons. It determined that in 1966, $39 million was spent by visitors, with 54 percent of that going to food and shelter. In 1998, it was determined that tourism brought in $125 million in economic benefit to Stratford. In 1951, there were eighteen restaurants in Stratford. By 1998, there were seventy-eight restaurants and 150 bed-and-breakfast facilities.

In an apparent effort to get the city in on the new restaurant and accommodation boom, Mayor C.H. Meier proposed in 1967 that city hall be moved from Market Place to 1 Ontario Street (where Victoria and Grey Trust bank was located), which would allow the city to redevelop the existing city hall site to include a round, ten-storey hotel with a revolving restaurant on top. He proudly displayed an artist's rendition of what appeared to be a complete eyesore, proposing that the historic and stately city hall be torn down and replaced with a building that would have more fit in with the 1960s futurist cartoon *The Jetsons*. Fortunately, this project never made it past the proposal stage, as citizens expressed their disdain for replacing city hall with such a behemoth.

Mayor C.H. Meier in 1967, proudly displaying an artist's rendition of his vision to tear down city hall and replace it with a ten-storey hotel with a rotating restaurant on the roof. *Stratford-Perth Archives*.

Interestingly, the theatre is also responsible for the development of the Ontario Street strip to the east of the downtown core, which is currently populated mostly with fast-food chain restaurants and motels. Visitors can easily come to Stratford to see the plays today without actually ever going downtown. Virtually every fast-food outlet from KFC to Arby's to Wendy's can be found along that strip, as well as some popular local family restaurants like Demetre's Family Eatery and Annie's Seafood Restaurant.

Stratford's reputation for marvelous restaurants was not earned until about twenty years after the festival was established. According to the great Christopher Plummer himself, saying that you wouldn't find a local restaurant listed in the *Gourmet* guide or with a Michelin star was putting it gently. His memories of being a hungry (and thirsty!) young thespian in Stratford were restricted to "good meat and veg" at the Queen's Inn, munching on egg rolls at the now-closed Chinese eatery the Golden Bamboo and getting banned from Ellam's all-night diner.

When Plummer found himself working with a cast that included many Quebecois, he finally experienced fantastic food in Stratford, as they cooked for him at their residences. "We would gorge on cassoulets, pizzaladiers, tourtieres, and boeuf bourguignons. At last there was a smell of garlic in the streets."

Plummer cites the term that Robin Phillips served as artistic director in the 1970s as the era when Stratford came to "rival any town in Canada in the art of *haute cuisine*," with the establishment of the Church Restaurant, Rundles and the Old Prune. Even the food that was served to the actors themselves saw dramatic improvement: "The Festival's Green Room, where once you were lucky to get a warmed-over hotdog and baked beans, now proudly offers confections of the highest order and some of the town's best grub!" Here's a little-known fact: cheesemaker Ruth Klahsen of Monforte Dairy fame was once the chef in the Green Room after graduating from the Stratford Chefs School.

Plummer has also indicated that his favourite place to go out for a bite and a drink after a long day of performing these days is Susan Dunfield's Down the Street restaurant, "a friendly *boite* full of wise saws and modern instances where gossip is king."

But without a doubt, there are three legendary restaurants that together have served to elevate the reputation of Stratford as a destination for people seeking unparalleled dining experiences: the Church Restaurant, the Old Prune and Rundles.

The Church Restaurant was established in 1975 by a renowned British restaurateur named Joe Mandel. Just over one hundred years earlier, in 1874, the Congressional Church had provided its first service in the newly completed church at the corner of Waterloo and Brunswick Streets. But a declining congregation took its toll, and in 1975, the building was deconsecrated and sold to Mr. Mandel, who renovated it into a spectacular restaurant replete with high cathedral ceilings and stained glass. The Church was quite simply *the* place to eat in Stratford in the 1970s and certainly raised the bar on the quality of food, service and sophistication found in the city's hospitality industry.

In 1988, the Church was purchased by Mark Craft, who began his career as a busboy at the restaurant before moving on to earn a degree in hotel administration from Ryerson University and seeing further hospitality industry success, including a stint as the manager of the Four Seasons in Calgary. He then returned to Stratford to take over the restaurant where he got his humble start, which now included a second restaurant, the Belfry, situated above the flagship dining room. Over the years, the menus at the Church have showcased local, organic ingredients in the hands of some of the best chefs in town. This included Chef Amédé Lamarche in the 2000s, who is now a head instructor at George Brown College's Chef School. Today, the kitchen is headed by Executive Chef Andrew Tutt, a native of Stratford and graduate of the Stratford Chefs School.

In 1976, two theatre lovers living in Montreal—Eleanor Kane and Marion Isherwood—visited Stratford to attend one of Robin Phillips's productions. On their way home on the train, they speculated on how great it would be if Stratford had a coffee bar or teashop, to which people could retire after the theatre to talk about the performances while enjoying some light refreshments. Mere weeks later, they were in Stratford looking for a suitable location for this spontaneous venture: neither of them had any experience in the hospitality industry, but they both knew that they were due for a change and that Stratford was the place they wanted to pursue it. In their explorations, they came across 151 Albert Street—a Victorian house slightly off the beaten path of downtown Stratford. They put in an offer that was accepted and proceeded to move to Stratford and transform their new property into a teahouse. They decided to name it after a nickname that had been jokingly bestowed on them by close friends, who had dubbed them the "old prunes."

The Old Prune opened its doors on May 10, 1977, and the teahouse was an immediate hit. People lined up down the block to get a table, and the two new restaurateurs personally cooked and served teas, sandwiches, salads, scones and cakes, all of which were made in house. Each took turns in the kitchen and dining room from week to week. However, soon each recognized her respective strengths, and Marion took over front of house, with Eleanor performing all the cooking.

With the support of the kitchen staff at the nearby Church Restaurant, who invited Eleanor to come and learn how to cook the kind of high-end food for which they were known, the Old Prune started providing dinners in addition to the lunches and teas that it had restricted itself to in the past. The operation began to expand, including the hiring of some new support staff. The wife of the chef at the brand-new Rundles restaurant, Sue Anderson, was hired to take on cooking duties, and the Old Prune soon blossomed into a full-on restaurant—not only serving lunch and dinner but also adding a post-theatre seating at 11:00 p.m., which would often keep staff busy until 2:00 a.m.! The seats were all full, and the business boomed.

The Old Prune at 151 Albert Street in 1984. It was established in a former Victorian home by Eleanor Kane and Marion Isherwood in 1977. *Stratford-Perth Archives.*

Sue Anderson stayed on as chef at the Old Prune for seven years, during which time the owners continued to renovate the building, adding new dining areas to accommodate the ever-increasing demand for their celebrated food. They became renowned not just among those who were visiting Stratford to see the shows but also among the actors who performed in them. By 1989, Eleanor had embarked on the parallel venture of using the restaurant during the off season as a teaching site for the Stratford Chefs School, which she was directing alongside Rundles owner Jim Morris. When the Old Prune hired Chef Bryan Steele to take on duties as chef in 1989, it also found itself a remarkable educator who continues to serve as chef instructor to this day. Steele's use of local ingredients to create distinctly Canadian cuisine was way ahead of its time when he started at the Old Prune, and today he is known as one of the best chefs in Ontario, if not Canada.

In 2010, after thirty-three years running the Old Prune, Marion and Eleanor decided that it was time to retire; today, it operates under different ownership as the Prune, but Chef Steele continues to provide Stratford visitors and residents with the kind of outstanding culinary experiences that served to put this city on the map among those who appreciate gourmet dining.

Certainly, however, a third restaurant also contributed significantly to the reputation that Stratford now enjoys as a culinary destination. Rundles was also established in 1977 as a joint venture between three theatre-loving Toronto housemates: James (Jim) Morris, Billy Munnelly and Marie Workman. Considering its current profile as a mecca for high-end, sophisticated cuisine, it is amusing to learn that the original concept sounds more like something associated with the Medieval Times experience, with a large dining hall complete with costumed serving wenches and court jesters providing entertainment. Having visited Stratford countless times and only finding the Church as a suitable destination for those seeking out a memorable dining experience, the trio knew that there was an opportunity. Fortunately, their plans to convert an old bowling alley into a medieval hall were changed when the site became unavailable, and instead they went ahead and pursued the dream of an artistic French eatery at a smaller location on Cobourg Street, overlooking the waters of the Avon River.

Deliberately, the three owners sought out a modern, minimalist aesthetic to contrast the opulence of the Church and the historical feel of the Old Prune. Over its first three seasons, the restaurant built a clientele and began to develop a reputation as an elegant, albeit high-

Rundles Restaurant on Cobourg Street in 1982, before extensive renovations featuring award-winning architecture. *Stratford-Perth Archives.*

priced, dining room. Billy Munnelly sold his share of the business to Jim and Marie after the third year of operation and moved on to establish the Rosedale Diner in Toronto. After a disappointing theatre season in 1981 and an even more discouraging restaurant season under an inferior new chef, Jim and Marie decided to promote their twenty-two-year-old British saucier to take over as chef. Neil Baxter proceeded to expand the menu at Rundles based on experience he gained staging (i.e., working for no salary) at some of the best Michelin star kitchens in France and New York during the restaurant's off season.

As the décor in Rundles became more refined, so, too, did the clientele. Included among those who have dined at Rundles are Canadian literary icons Margaret Atwood, Alice Munro and Robertson Davies, who declared that Rundles was his favourite place to eat in the world. In 1987, Marie decided that the highly refined vibe at Rundles was more suitable to Jim's preferences than her own, and Jim bought her out to become the sole proprietor of the restaurant. He proceeded to add an addition on the back of the building to accommodate an expanded kitchen and added an upper story, where he would soon come to reside.

Jim continues to run Rundles, and the Stratford Chefs School continues to use the restaurant as a classroom and teaching kitchen in the off season. Over thirty years since being promoted to executive chef, Neil Baxter maintains the highest standards of culinary excellence in the restaurant, which now also includes a separate bistro section for those seeking out a slightly more modest menu. Over time, Jim Morris has pursued further enhancements to the building itself, with an ambitious renovation undertaken between 1999 and 2002 that saw the addition of a guesthouse, the Rundles Morris House. Today, the architecture of Rundles is as celebrated as the food, and it maintains its high standards in service, décor and cuisine to the acclaim of critics and loyal patrons alike.

The list of restaurants worth mentioning in Stratford today goes on and on. From the house-made charcuterie at the Mercer Hall wine bar (recently named one of the top one hundred restaurants in Canada by vacay.ca) to the authentic Italian fare at Pazzo Taverna and Ristorante, the French cuisine of Rene's Bistro and the creative fusion of Bijou (or the Bruce Restaurant, where the former chef/owners of Bijou now run the show), there is no shortage of places to go for those who love good food. For those seeking out a pub lunch or a takeout picnic, there are multiple spots where quality local ingredients are used to create crowd-pleasing dishes, including the Olde English Parlour, Molly Bloom's Irish pub, the County Food Co. and York Street Kitchen.

In 2013, the theme of the Savour Stratford Perth County Culinary Festival was "International Goes Local," which was fitting because there have never been more opportunities for people to eat food from diverse cultures in the city than today. The Golden Bamboo was a landmark Chinese food eatery serving egg rolls and chicken balls to patrons and actors of the Stratford Festival, as well as to chow mein–loving residents; it has been closed now for over a decade. Still going strong, Gene's Restaurant has been serving Chinese food to the Stratford community since 1970. It moved from its location on Erie Street, where Larry and Rae Gene operated a dining room with thirty-five seats, to its present location on Ontario Street, where their son, Ken Gene, continues to serve Cantonese and Szechuan specialties. For those seeking Japanese food, there is Pearl Sushi on Downie Street, but those in the know will tell you that the best Japanese food in town is actually prepared fresh on the spot by a Korean man known as Mr. Kim at his General Store on Ontario Street. Students from Stratford Central High School swarm his counter every lunch hour as he rolls maki after maki to sell to these fish-loving teenagers. There is also Indian food available at Raja and around the corner at the Taj buffet, as well as two locations that serve Thai food.

Bentley's is a favourite place for locals and tourists to go when out for a drink or two and a bite to eat; you might even spot the mayor of Stratford there on a Friday evening having a beer and a snack after a long week of running the city. The sign over the door did not always bear the name of the owner Breen Bentley; he started as a busboy when the place was called the Jester Arms, owned by David Lester. Famous as a late-night post-theatre hangout for actors as well as attendees from the Stratford Shakespeare Festival—patrons included Maggie Smith, Peter Ustinov and Robin Phillips—the British pub-themed watering hole would be packed every night with people drinking draught beer and eating roast beef dinners. When Breen Bentley (who had attended the Stratford Chefs School in the interim between working as a busboy and buying the place) took over, there was one condition. Lester would finance the mortgage, but Bentley couldn't change a thing—including the name of the establishment—until every penny was paid off. The day he made his last payment, Breen Bentley removed the sign bearing the "Jester Arms" name and proudly replaced it with "Bentley's."

Justin Bieber's favourite place to eat during his childhood in his hometown of Stratford was Madelyn's Diner; opened in 1985 by Madelyn McCarty, today it is run by her daughter, Krista Moore. In addition to being a great place for breakfast, Madelyn's is known for inventive buttertart creations, including garlic buttertarts and bacon buttertarts.

Foster's Inn carries on the old tradition of downtown Stratford hotels that also serve great food and is known as a place to get a good steak. And if you're looking for a place to have some good food and a cocktail, you might just run into Christopher Plummer on the patio at Down the Street.

Stratford has certainly come a long way from an outpost where one was lucky to find cucumbers pickled in whisky, greasy steaks and peas served in a washbasin. Now it is a destination where one has multiple options for the finest of dining experiences. Driven by the success of the Stratford Shakespeare Festival, the many restaurants in town also create a ripple effect that supports the success of local agriculture, provides jobs for many Stratford residents and young people and draws food lovers to the community.

Chapter 6

The Stratford Chefs School

By the early 1980s, the burgeoning restaurant scene in Stratford was experiencing some growing pains. The first was a lack of highly trained chefs with the skills and knowledge necessary to meet the increasing demand for fine dining experiences at Stratford's three high-end restaurants: the Old Prune, Rundles and the Church. In order to maintain their lofty standards of cuisine, owners would often find themselves needing to recruit culinary talent from Europe. The second was the seasonal nature of Stratford's tourism industry, which saw restaurants booked solid for two or three seatings a night during the Stratford Shakespeare Festival season and zero traffic between the months from November to April. For six months of the year, these beautiful restaurants, with their top-notch kitchens, were closed and sitting idle, their expert chefs twiddling their thumbs waiting for the next theatre season to arrive. Third, other Stratford restaurants like the Olde English Parlour and the Jester Arms Pub Restaurant and Hotel wanted their cooking staff to upgrade their skills, but the only place to take chef training at that time in Ontario was George Brown College in Toronto; when cooks from Stratford went there to study and apprentice, they rarely came back.

In 1983, a man named John Evans, who was the manager of the Stratford Employment Centre, called together a meeting of Stratford restaurateurs. Jim Morris, who at that time was a co-owner of Rundles, and Eleanor Kane, co-owner of the Old Prune, were in attendance. The discussion confirmed that the restaurant owners were motivated to

The inaugural class of the Stratford Chefs School outside the Church Restaurant. Chefs in training are in white, with Joe Mandel (left), Eleanor Kane (centre) and James Morris (right) flanking the sign. *Private collection of Terry Manzo.*

Jim Morris (left, wearing bowtie) and Eleanor Kane (right) mentoring early student chefs at the Stratford Chefs School. *Private collection of Terry Manzo.*

Fred and Ingrid Demartines from Perth Pork Products, with a wild boar head, alongside bearded Mercer Hall chefs Sean Collins (left) and Tim Larsen (right) at the 2013 Savour Stratford Perth County Culinary Festival's Sunday Tasting Tent. *Stratford Tourism Alliance.*

Tina Vandenheuvel and Antony John out in the fields at Soiled Reputation Organic Farm. In the background, a team of workers picks their famous greens. *Stratford Tourism Alliance.*

Luann and Tim Erb and sons on the tractor at Erbcroft Farm. The mixed farm includes duck, lamb and a resident llama. *Stratford Tourism Alliance.*

Warren Ham from August's Harvest Farm outside Gadshill, grower of organic garlic and Saskatoon berries. Farmer Ham was a founder of the Stratford Garlic Festival. *Stratford Tourism Alliance.*

In May 2012, the Slow Food Sunday Market launched its outdoor season in Market Square alongside a Food Trucks Eats, a gathering of food trucks from around the province. Local restaurants also operated pop-up stands to feed the hungry masses. *Stratford Tourism Alliance.*

Chef Ryan O'Donnell (on right) teaching Stratford Chefs School students in the kitchen of the Prune Restaurant, where he also works as sous chef. *Stratford Tourism Alliance.*

Above: Toronto celebrity chef Jamie Kennedy (right) teaching culinary arts students at the Screaming Avocado Café. *From the* Stratford Beacon Herald.

Left: Paul Finkelstein in a promotional piece for the Food Network Canada show *Fink!*. *Frantic Films.*

The riverside farmers' market at the Savour Stratford Perth County Culinary Festival. *Stratford Tourism Alliance.*

Stratford's own Darren Dumas, frontman for aptly named band the Salads, performs at the Savour Stratford Perth County Culinary Festival. *Stratford Tourism Alliance.*

Top Chef Canada champion and Stratford Chefs School grad Chef Carl Heinrich, *Top Chef Canada* finalist and chef/owner of Charcut restaurant in Calgary Connie DeSousa, Savour Stratford Perth County Culinary Festival founder Danielle Brodhagen and David Rocco from Food Network Canada's *Dolce Vida*. *Stratford Tourism Alliance.*

Left to right: Joe Lass, son of Mark Lass from Lassdale Farm, paired with Craig Foster from Foster's Inn at the 2012 Savour Stratford Perth County Sunday Tasting Tent. *Stratford Tourism Alliance.*

Vancouver celebrity chef Vikram Vij at The Local Community Food Centre for the GE Café Chefs Series at the 2013 Savour Stratford Perth County Culinary Festival. *Stratford Tourism Alliance.*

The Local Community Food Centre's chef/educator Jordan Lassaline preparing the Monday community dinner with volunteers. *The Local Community Food Centre.*

Baby spinach and beetroot salad finished with local goats cheese chèvre and walnuts. Chef Max Holbrook, 2011. *Stratford Tourism Alliance.*

Down the Street Restaurant, a popular patio for locals and visitors to get a drink along with some fabulous food. *Stratford Tourism Alliance.*

Fresh local produce for sale at the Savour Stratford Perth County Culinary Festival farmers'
market. *Stratford Tourism Alliance.*

Katrina McQuail from Meeting Place Organics embracing a bucket of basil at the Savour
Stratford Perth County Culinary Festival. *Stratford Tourism Alliance.*

Way-finding at the Savour Stratford Perth County Culinary Festival. *Stratford Tourism Alliance.*

York Street during the Savour Stratford Perth County Culinary Festival. *Stratford Tourism Alliance.*

The Screaming Avocado Café's vending station at the 2010 Savour Stratford Perth County Culinary Festival, where it sold Three Sisters Soup featuring corn, beans and squash grown via the Stratford School Gardens project. *Stratford Tourism Alliance.*

Left to right: Susan Dunfield, owner of Down the Street Restaurant; Soiled Reputation Farm's Antony "the Manic Organic" John; and Chef Lee Avigdor at the Savour Stratford Perth County Culinary Festival Sunday Tasting Tent. *Stratford Tourism Alliance.*

Chicken butchery demonstration by the Healthy Butcher at the Savour Stratford Perth County Culinary Festival. *Stratford Tourism Alliance.*

Muffuletta Sandwich, pork done six ways: coppa, rillette, prosciutto, country ham, black-strap molasses ham and pig's head mortadella. Mercer Hall chef Tim Larsen, winner of Best Meat Dish at the 2012 Savour Stratford Sunday Tasting Tent. *Stratford Tourism Alliance.*

Liz Mountain and Elizabeth Anderson from The Local Community Food Centre assemble pigtail terrine by Chef Jordan Lassaline for the 2013 Savour Stratford Sunday Tasting Tent. *Stratford Tourism Alliance.*

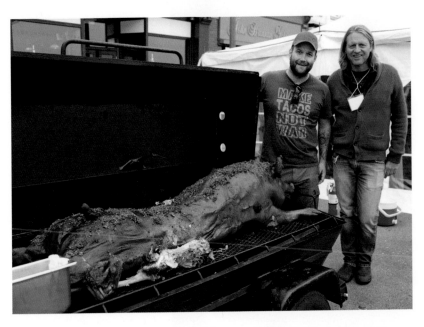

Whole pig roasted by Nick Benninger, chef/owner of Nick and Nat's Uptown 21 and Taco Farm in Waterloo. The pig was raised by Mark Lass (right) from Lassdale Farm and was fed a special diet of apples and herbs for the Savour Stratford Sunday Tasting. *Stratford Tourism Alliance.*

Above: Mark Lass from Lassdale Farm (left) along with Foster's Inn owner Craig Foster (right) and team at the Savour Stratford Sunday Tasting Tent. *Stratford Tourism Alliance.*

Left: Savoury tart featuring local beets, cheese and fresh thyme. Down the Street chef Lee Avigdor, 2012. *Stratford Tourism Alliance.*

Handmade ravioli featuring Monforte Toscano cheese and local shiitakes with Tamworth bacon and organic pea shoots. Pazzo Taverna chef Yva Santini, 2013. *Stratford Tourism Alliance.*

French sticks by Downie Street Bakehouse at the Slow Food Sunday Market. *Stratford Tourism Alliance.*

increase the supply of pastry chefs, sauciers, chefs de cuisine and executive chefs for their kitchens. It also became clear that they were interested in making their restaurants, staff and equipment available during the off season to address that problem.

As it happened, Morris had for a while been contemplating creating a program to train executive chefs for employment at his upscale restaurant. But he knew that he couldn't do it alone. After that meeting, he and Eleanor Kane reached out to Joe Mandel, owner of the Church, as well as Conestoga College's manager of planning. The management of the Olde English Parlour and the Jester Arms Pub Restaurant and Hotel also got involved. Together, they all set out to create a unique chef training program in Stratford that would make good use of its dormant restaurants during the off season to train chefs of the future for the city's restaurant community.

There were other educational institutions at that time training people for careers in cooking. However, with the exception of George Brown College, all of these focused on teaching techniques for cooking institutional food on a large scale such as those found in hospitals. The artistry and technique required to elevate cuisine to the level of fine dining was something that the Stratford restaurateurs were finding in short supply, and they set out to do something about it.

Just as a great chef produces all of his or her dishes from scratch and with personal care and attention, so too did Jim Morris create the curriculum for the Stratford Chefs School based on his own knowledge of what it took to achieve culinary excellence. He spent three months writing an original training and apprentice program involving six thousand hours of both practical instruction in restaurant kitchens and classroom content. He wanted the chefs to know every element involved in the achievement of an unforgettable dining experience from top to bottom. This included instruction on nutrition, sanitation, wine appreciation, presentation, ingredient sourcing, aesthetics and restaurant financials. Just as importantly, the course was designed to give participants the opportunity to create a culinary style of their own based on their personal opinions and preferences. They were not being trained as automatons to blindly reproduce classical dishes by rote but were rather encouraged to apply their own creativity to various techniques with the goal of developing their distinctive personal character as a chef. Teaching the basics of cooking, with focused attention on detail and the highest standards of ingredients, would prepare the chefs in training at the Stratford Chefs School to eventually perform at the level of the best chefs working in world-class restaurants in New York or San Francisco.

To deliver this one-of-a-kind course, the best talents in Kane's and Morris's restaurants were called on to come out of their winter hibernation and get back into the kitchen to teach. The cooking instructors for the first class of the Stratford Chefs School were Chris Woolf, then a chef at Rundles, and Sue Anderson, chef at the Old Prune. Bill Munnelly, a Stratford wine consultant, taught the students wine appreciation—an area of chef studies that was unique to the Stratford program. Morris himself taught the sections on sourcing commodities and produce buying. Kane taught her own specialties: gastronomy and nutrition. Chinese cooking expert Ella Yoa was invited to come from Toronto to teach Asian cookery. Business and accounting was taught by Joe Mandel from the Church. Finally, a retired gallery manager and artist named Robert Ihrig was enlisted to teach food styling.

It was necessary that the classes be kept small, as the kitchen at Rundles could only fit eight cooks at a time, so the first batch of trainee chefs numbered only sixteen specially selected students in the inaugural year. In November 1983, they began the process of training to become certified chefs under the apprenticeship program offered through Conestoga College out of Kitchener. This involved two fifteen-week periods of classroom and kitchen instruction during the winter and 4,500 hours of on-the-job training working in Stratford restaurants. To officially become a certified chef, students would then have to pass an examination.

The Stratford Chefs School therefore emerged out of an unprecedented cooperative effort between provincial and federal employment programs, an established educational institution and a private-sector restaurant community whose leaders recognized that if they all worked together, it would benefit the entire sector and create a truly remarkable culinary scene—all in the unlikely setting of an Ontario town with only thirty thousand people.

For its first four years, the school operated as a division of Conestoga College in partnership with the federal Human Resources and Development Canada jobs program and the Ontario Ministry of Education and Training on the provincial level. It was then established as a standalone not-for-profit educational institution—the only food preparatory school that was not part of a community college operating with the funding support of Ministry of Skills Development. Tuition costs were kept down in contrast to comparable institutions like the

Culinary Institute of America through ministry funding (providing about half of the school's annual budget), with the rest coming from a diverse fundraising program that included corporate sponsorships and culinary events.

Enrollment in the program increased over time. The second year saw the student body jump from sixteen to twenty-two chefs in training. By 1989, there were thirty-nine students, which grew to sixty-four by 1991. By 2000, there were seventy spots available in total for both the first- and second-year programs. Most impressively, by 2000, the Stratford Chefs School was able to boast a 100 percent placement rate for its students in the kitchens of Stratford and the rest of the world.

The problems that had inspired the initiation of the school—a lack of talented, well-trained chefs in Stratford and a culinary off season that was completely dead—had been conquered. In 2000, there were at least fifteen restaurants in Stratford that were either owned by Stratford Chefs School graduates or had chefs who were graduates leading their kitchen teams. The winter months saw a whole new phenomenon of near daily lunches and dinners prepared by students as part of their training. Five dinners a week and two lunches represented the hands-on course work on which students were graded, and community members were all invited to come taste for themselves the products of the students' education for a very reasonable price. Students were responsible not only for cooking the food but also for preparing the restaurant, serving the food and wine and communicating the menus to patrons. The student meals emulated the experience of working in the restaurants in which they were learning— the Old Prune and Rundles—with their chefs serving as the instructors.

Over time, the Stratford Chefs School became more than just a place where aspiring chefs from Stratford, Canada and beyond could learn their chops; it became a force for promoting the very concept of a Canadian cuisine—an elusive and often neglected area of our country's cultural heritage. In 1993, on the tenth anniversary of the Chefs School's launch, the city of Stratford was host to a three-day conference entitled Northern Bounty, where 60 experts and 150 delegates explored and celebrated the characteristics that made Canadian food unique as a culinary tradition. Chefs School students served one of the conference meals at Knox Church—dubbed the Order of the Good Cheer Banquet, it honoured Samuel de Champlain's seventeenth-century gastronomical society and was embellished by props and costumes from the Stratford Shakespeare Festival. Conference sessions included discussions on the sustainability of the farming sector in Canada, standards in the Canadian restaurant industry, marketing traditional native and distinctively Canadian food and agricultural products and the mingling of diverse international culinary traditions within the profile of contemporary Canadian cuisine.

The Stratford Chefs School experience is a unique one for students, as they immerse themselves in intensive classroom instruction while also taking on restaurant cooking duties on a daily basis. The structure of the school is small and intimate, and as in any restaurant, it requires cooperation and interaction between students if they hope to be successful. Strong relationships are created among fellow students working closely with one another, as well as between students and their faculty mentors over the two-year instructional period. These characteristics, mixed with the demanding curriculum and the high expectations placed on students, is a recipe for drama—it led one Stratford Chefs School grad to approach Food Network Canada and pitch the idea of filming a "docu-soap" following a class of students over their two years at SCS.

The show was picked up, and in 2006 a group of first-year students had the additional factors of lights, cameras and microphones accompanying their educational experience. The show was called *Chef School* and, like any soap opera, featured a range of character depictions, from the chartered accountant reinventing herself by following her passion for food and cooking to the reformed addict who finds salvation in the restaurant kitchen and the volatile local boy who refuses to accept criticism from even the most revered experts in the industry. Chef instructors Neil Baxter and Bryan Steele are presented as difficult-to-please task masters, with the action punctuated by wise narratives courtesy of co-directors Eleanor Kane and Jim Morris.

Chef School premiered on January 1, 2008, with thirteen episodes following twelve students through their first-year ordeals. By the second season, the group had been trimmed down to nine soon-to-be chefs. The show was met with high ratings and critical praise and even managed to win the 2008 Gemini Award for Best Lifestyle/Practical Information Series. The Stratford Chefs School enjoyed unparalleled exposure through the widely aired series and saw immediate increases in applications and enrollment. The special learning environment that had been cultivating high-level chef talent in Stratford for twenty-five years was now a TV drama that people were following in their living rooms.

Taping the Food Network Canada television series *Chef School*, which documented a class at the Stratford Chefs School over two years. The show went on to win a Gemini Award. *From the* Stratford Beacon Herald.

That same year, the Stratford Chefs School introduced another communications program designed to assist the student chefs in expressing themselves and their cuisine through the written word. Joseph Hoare was a former food editor for *Toronto Life* magazine who was known for encouraging young food writers before his unfortunate death in 1997. To commemorate him and carry on his vision of a distinctive Canadian food culture supported by strong writing, his family set up the Joseph Hoare Gastronomic Writer in Residence Program at the Stratford Chefs School.

The first writer in residence under this program was acclaimed Canadian food writer James Chatto, who had begun his food writing career with *Toronto Life* at the encouragement of Joseph Hoare, even though he had no writing experience. He went on to win multiple awards for his books and restaurant criticism and became senior editor and consultant for the popular LCBO publication *Food and Drink*. In 2008, he came to Stratford for twelve days, during which time he met one on one with students to help them hone their writing skills, delivered a food writing workshop for the public and observed firsthand the classes and dinners in which the students were participating.

In 2009, the writer in residence was Corby Krummer, American Slow Food advocate and James Beard Journalism Award winner who was well known as a contributor to the culinary columns of the *New York Magazine*, *Atlantic Monthly* and *Boston Magazine*, as well as author of several books. In 2010, the invitation was extended to the esteemed Australian food writer and historian Michael Symons. The year 2011 saw Ian Brown, an award-winning Canadian nonfiction author whose writings on food were published in a *Globe and Mail* series entitled "Ian Brown Eats Canada," serve as writer in residence, offering a well-attended reading at the Stratford Public Library as well as the one-on-one sessions and workshops. In 2012, the Chefs School broadened its recognition of culinary writing to include food bloggers, inviting Parisian Clotilde Desoulier of the English-language blog Chocolate & Zucchini to come share insights and literary techniques with students and the Stratford community. James Oseland, editor of the industry-leading *Saveur* magazine, served in the position in 2013. The 2014 Gastronomic writer in residence was Canadian Dianne Jacob, author of the multiple-award-winning cookbook *Will Write for Food*; her tenure also included a free public reading in Stratford, as well as a writing workshop conducted in Toronto.

The Stratford Chefs School's Gastronomic Writer in Residence Program reflects and supports its goal to provide students with a well-rounded educational experience; not only are they prepared in techniques for cooking and serving great food, but they are also equipped with the tools they need to communicate their culinary experiences and dishes as provided by some of the best writers in this country and internationally.

Thirty years since it began, the Stratford Chefs School has set the benchmark for quality culinary education in Canada and beyond. The long list of visiting chefs who have come to Stratford to tutor the students demonstrates the quality of the instruction they have received. Canadian celebrity chefs include Susur Lee, Chris MacDonald, Michael Stadtlander and Jamie Kennedy. International chefs have come to train classes in French, Italian, Mexican, Asian and other world cuisines and have included stars such as Australia's Ben Shewry of Attica Restaurant in Melbourne and French Michelin star–winning chef Alexandre Gauthier.

Over time, its alumni and coordinators have also received extensive accolades and awards. In 2012, SCS class of 2005 grad Carl Heinrich won the Food Network's *Top Chef Canada* competition and went on to use his winnings to start up the acclaimed Richmond Station restaurant in Toronto along with fellow Stratford Chefs School graduate Ryan

Broadcaster Peter Mansbridge and his wife, actor Cynthia Dale, two of Stratford's most prominent citizens, introduce the Culinary Family Tree at the 2012 Savour Stratford Perth County Culinary Festival. *Stratford Tourism Alliance.*

Donovan. James Morris was awarded the Ontario Hostelry Institute's Gold Award for Outstanding Contribution to the Hospitality and Service Industry of Ontario. Eleanor Kane was also awarded the Gold Award for Outstanding Contribution by the Ontario Hostelry Institute in 2001, and in 2012, just before stepping down from the coordinator position she held for twenty-nine years, Kane was recognized by her peers as the Woman of the Year by the Toronto Women's Culinary Network.

There is a saying: "The best time to plant a tree is thirty years ago... or today." A Stratford Culinary Family Tree was created in 2012 for the Savour Stratford Perth County Culinary Festival and demonstrated pictorially how the seeds that were planted thirty years ago by Kane and Morris have blossomed into far-reaching branches that include many of the brightest lights in Stratford's restaurant kitchens. This includes local culinary leaders like Aaron and Bronwyn Linley, former owners of Bijou who have moved on to run the Bruce Restaurant; Yva Santini of Pazzo's Taverna; Breen Bentley, owner of Bentley's; and Monforte Dairy cheesemaker Ruth Klahsen. Indeed, the tree could have easily been depicted extending not just throughout Stratford but also throughout the province: Jeff Crump, corporate chef at the Ancaster Mill, is recognized as one of the pioneers of Slow Food in Ontario through his passion for locally grown, seasonal ingredients.

The year 2014 marks the thirtieth anniversary of the culmination of the Stratford Chefs School's first season, and it has certainly achieved everything the founders had hoped it would. Expert chefs trained at the Chefs School now populate almost every restaurant kitchen in Stratford, and the days of importing culinary talent from Europe are long past.

Chapter 7

The Screaming Avocado Café

The Screaming Avocado Café is the "alternative cafeteria," where Stratford Northwestern Secondary School's culinary arts teacher Paul Finkelstein teaches students how to cook by letting them create and serve lunch to their classmates and teachers every day. Justin Bieber ate there almost every day while he was attending the middle school at Northwestern. You might think that would be its claim to fame, but in fact, the Screaming Avocado has received tremendous attention and accolades for its hands-on model designed to provide students with real-world experience in a restaurant environment while also preparing them for a lifetime of cooking from scratch, food systems awareness and appreciation of the power of food to bring people together.

In this case, that power is applied to their whole school: every day, there is a lineup out the door for fantastic meals sold for only three dollars per heaping plate. In cases where students can't afford the three dollars, they eat all the same; young Justin Bieber could often be found at a back table—surrounded by fawning classmates while counting the thousands of hits he was racking up on YouTube and eating a meal he was provided free of charge because he had shown up with empty pockets. But it wasn't Bieber who attracted the attention of the national newspapers, *Time* magazine, *Saveur* and producers from Food Network Canada; feeding the Biebs didn't bring the Screaming Avocado class to the James Beard House in New York City or to cook for Will and Kate at Rideau Hall in Ottawa. Even the Prime Minister of Canada, who wasn't aware that culinary arts was taught in Canadian high schools, eventually came to recognize the success of the Screaming Avocado Café was due to the visionary teaching (and cooking) excellence of its founder, Paul Finkelstein.

But Finkelstein was not always known for educational excellence, especially when he was around the age of the students he teaches today. Bright but not highly motivated to thrive in a normal classroom setting, he recalls a time when food sparked his own ability to learn in an unconventional way. In grade eight, his class went to the museum in Toronto, and he noticed all the skeletons of the animals and fossils and how their bones were held together with wire. Intent on reproducing this upon his return to school, his teacher allowed him to take on a special project: the next week, he was in the school courtyard with a whole chicken from the grocery store, a Bunsen burner and a pot. He attempted to boil the chicken down to get to its bones and re-create the skeletal models he had observed at the museum. In the end, he didn't figure out how to put the chicken back together again…but he had learned how to make chicken stock.

Cooking was something he had become comfortable with at an early age, having cooked for himself on a daily basis while his mother went to work. That turned into him cooking in restaurants as he journeyed through Canada and the world as a young man. He wound up in Kingston, Ontario, where he spent many more than the typical three years working on a BA degree at Queen's University. All the while, he cooked at restaurants, which eventually brought him into contact with several graduates from the Stratford Chefs School. One Chefs School alumnus who owned a restaurant where he was working encouraged him to pursue his chefs training in Stratford.

That mentor brought him for a visit to Stratford to experience the Stratford Chefs School in person. To this day, Finkelstein remembers the smell of the kitchen at Rundles and is reminded of his first visit every time he steps into Jim Morris's Stratford restaurant. He was able to sit in on some classes and do some cooking alongside the chefs in training. He immediately fell in love with the idea of attending the Chefs School himself. The next day, he was able to tag along on a field trip to the acclaimed Mildred Pierce restaurant in Toronto, where the students were invited to eat and then reflect on the experience by writing their own restaurant reviews. He got to meet the chefs at the restaurant and get introduced to a whole different side of food: the art of cooking pursued at a higher level than he had ever witnessed before.

He was enrolled as a student chef the following October. His wife, Amanda, who herself was entering into her second year of Chefs School at the time Paul first arrived, recalls how everyone was talking about some "crazy guy" who would get up at five o'clock in the morning and go to Tim Hortons to study before class. Paul was that "crazy guy." Like many others who attended the Stratford Chefs School at that time (the year was 1995), he wasn't just coming out of high school and jumping straight into chef training: many were older and looking at reinventing themselves or finding their true calling. Completely immersing himself into all things culinary was Finkelstein's response to discovering his real passion—he had finally found what he wanted to do in life and threw himself in 100 percent.

The motivation to work hard at Chefs School was also associated with job opportunities in Stratford at that time. Rundles and the Old Prune would each only hire one person per year once the school season ended and the restaurant and festival season kicked off, so there was a lot of competition among students to achieve in the classroom so they could win one of these prized kitchen positions. At that time, high-end restaurants weren't as numerous in Stratford as they are today, so there were limited options for budding chefs. Paul was rewarded for his hard work when he was invited to join Bryan Steele's team at the Old Prune that summer. The following summer, after another year of superlative educational performance, he was actually invited to join Stratford Chefs School founders Eleanor Kane and Jim Morris on a trip to Europe as their personal chef.

Paul and Amanda got married immediately after he finished Chefs School in 1997. Then, like several other entrepreneurial graduates of the SCS at that time who felt that there was room for more great restaurants in Stratford, Paul went on to start his own place, Moxie's, in partnership with another SCS grad. It was a fine time to open a restaurant in Stratford—the Canadian dollar was low compared to the American dollar, and this brought countless tourists to the Stratford Shakespeare Festival. The seats at Moxie's were always full for lunch and dinner, and the endeavour was financially successful. The partners bought the place next door and opened a bakery, with Amanda coming on board to run that side of the operation. But the work was extremely hard when the season was in full swing, and in the off season, it was slow and therefore difficult to sustain both sides of the partnership. Amanda gave birth to their first child, and they sold the restaurant and bakery to the partner.

The new family returned to Kingston to run a restaurant for another fellow Chefs School alumnus. Then one day Paul was in the kitchen when he heard one of the staff chefs say that she was applying to the teachers college at Queen's to teach foods in high schools. In a life-changing moment, Paul asked, "They teach foods in high schools!?" He went to the Queen's Faculty of Education the next morning to get more information and to confirm that culinary studies was indeed a high school teachable, and later that day, he visited a Kingston high school to see for himself a culinary arts program in action. He applied to teachers college the next day and was ultimately accepted.

Paul thrived in teachers college based on his ability to bring what he had learned at Stratford Chefs School into focus in his assignments. In particular, he had studied the work of Alice Waters, the California founder of the Edible Schoolyard, which he knew he wanted to apply to his teaching practice wherever he ended up. At his first teaching placement in a Kingston high school, he was disappointed to find that the students were learning how to cook in the school cafeteria, where all the food was deep fried and prefabricated. In those days, before the push for better nutrition in Ontario schools, this was how students were taught how to run a food service business: they raised funds for their programs by doing exactly what all the fast-food franchises they were competing with were doing. Paul pushed back on this and took a few students to the side every day to create culturally diverse specials cooked from scratch. He knew that he couldn't run a classroom out of a conventional school cafeteria; when he graduated, he put together a proposal for the school board in Kingston to let him run a "seed to table"–style program with a farm partnership component. It was rejected, and he found that there were no jobs for a teacher with his kind of vision in Kingston.

He was offered a teaching position in Brantford with the promise that he could immediately install gardens on the school grounds for students to grow food for their culinary arts programs. But while this was exactly what he was looking for, housing was in short supply in that community, so Paul and Amanda returned to Stratford, where Paul had been offered a position at Stratford Northwestern Secondary School. To his great fortune, the leadership at the school was undergoing a wholesale change, with a new principal, Deb McNair, coming on board at the same time he was starting at the school. She proved to be a fellow visionary and a true champion of Finkelstein's innovative approach to teaching culinary arts.

Together they started a foods program at the school on a small budget. Paul quickly learned that his students were not taking his class because they necessarily wanted to become chefs; they were taking it because they wanted to learn how to cook good food. Approaching their education at an advanced level would have been foolish in Finkelstein's eyes, so he started with the basics.

Even at that level, he immediately realized that the cost for buying ingredients for the lessons would exceed the funds that were available. So the class started selling food they'd cooked across the hall to teachers in the staff room. They'd sell pots of soup with scones, and that was his students' first venture into making money from what they were cooking. They started selling fifteen to twenty bowls of soup a day, which would earn them the forty dollars they would need for their lesson's ingredients the next day.

After a month of brisk soup sales, the people who ran the cafeteria caught wind of these transactions and pulled out their contract with the school board that stated that no one could sell food on school grounds during cafeteria hours other than them. Even though the culinary arts students were only selling soup to teachers, they were shut down. Paul and Deb agreed this was wrong and that something had to change.

Initially, they got around the situation by selling frozen soup to teachers after cafeteria hours so they could heat it up themselves. This evolved into the students selling their delicious frozen soups to teachers across all the elementary schools in Stratford.

The students earned more revenue through their cooking by taking on catering gigs. Then they initiated a Culinary Club, serving fundraiser dinners to support class trips, the first of which took them to New York City for six days of visiting culinary programs in that city, as well as some of its best restaurants. As the club evolved and the program kept growing, it was evident that it would need a bigger space. Principal Deb, who was aware that the cafeteria contract was coming up the following year, took over a large space in the school that was formerly used for teaching printing and printmaking and had it transformed into the kitchen classroom that would become the Screaming Avocado Café.

Deb and Paul negotiated upon the renewal of the cafeteria contract to allow for the culinary arts classroom to cook and serve lunch to sell to students and staff. The cafeteria managers probably underestimated the capacity for Paul and his students to cater to the lunchtime crowd at the school board's largest school—they didn't expect them to open up what very much resembled a full-on restaurant! But by the time the cafeteria managers realized that they had serious competition, it was too late to change the agreement.

And so the Screaming Avocado Café was born. Soon there were bright colours on all the walls and loud music coming out of the PA speakers. Paul's teaching format changed to the benefit of the learners, as they were able to cook for a three-hour double-credit class over the entire morning, gaining consistency by cooking right through to the end of increasingly complex dishes. Kids who were not even students in the class were welcome to come help serve at lunch, sometimes because they felt they needed a safe space and other times because they didn't get a good lunch from home and felt empowered to help out after being offered a free meal. The students were given the opportunity to decide on what was going to be served on the menu, and Finkelstein—now known lovingly as "Fink" among his student kitchen team—was able to teach them all sorts of techniques based on their ideas.

Before long, Paul had fulfilled his vision of a Canadian version of the Edible Schoolyard with the creation of a four-thousand-square-foot organic garden established in the courtyard just down the hall from his classroom. The students weren't just cooking the food they were serving; they were growing it too!

It didn't take long for this remarkable story—the first school in Canada where a student-run restaurant was going head to head with the cafeteria— to catch the attention of the media. The local *Beacon Herald* newspaper had been coming out to Culinary Club dinners and following Fink's work and was soon celebrating the innovative educational experience at the Screaming Avocado. Marion Kane, one of the country's top food writers, did an article for the *Toronto Star*. The *Globe and Mail* featured Fink and the Screaming Avocado in a piece on the unhealthiness of typical school lunch fare: the whole country learned that when given the option between fried junk food and wholesome lunches cooked from scratch, many students at Northwestern picked the healthier option every day. This, in turn, led to an article published in the prominent American food magazine *Saveur* contrasting this program to the typical American high school food experience, with *Time* magazine publishing a similar piece. High-profile food personalities started coming to the Screaming Avocado to work with Paul's students, including chefs Jamie Kennedy, Michael Stadtlander and Christine Cushing, along with local culinary stars like

Antony "the Manic Organic" John and Monforte Dairy cheesemaker Ruth Klahsen.

At that time, a freelancer from *Canadian Living* magazine arrived to do a piece on the Screaming Avocado. She was also a producer for Food Network Canada. Fifteen minutes after she arrived, she came up to Paul and said, "This is a TV show."

Paul and the production team from Food Network Canada spent Christmas creating the storyline for a thirteen-episode documentary series entitled *Fink!*. One episode would follow a student who had never cooked at home as he created a meal for his family based on what he'd learned at the Screaming Avocado. Another would see the Avocado team travelling to Toronto to help cook and serve a community meal at a homeless shelter. Two episodes would follow the Culinary Arts club on a trip to Italy, where the students would tour various culinary destinations and end up at the Slow Food Terra Madre festival.

When the Christmas break was over, the Screaming Avocado Café was transformed into a film set with a crew of fifteen following the class over four months. Although the producers might have been disappointed that Fink wasn't the kind of Gordon Ramsay–style tyrant that was becoming the model for food reality TV, that semester saw a particularly extraordinary group of young people learning at the Avocado. If students didn't want to be featured on camera, their wishes were always respected.

And so the remarkable story of the Screaming Avocado Café at Stratford's Northwestern Secondary School became forever immortalized in a Food Network Canada classic. Fink has since gained a reputation as "Canada's Jamie Oliver" for his outstanding work and is widely recognized as a groundbreaking innovator for his successes in empowering young people to care about their food, how it's cooked, where it comes from and who controls it.

One student in particular from the *Fink!* series—a young man named Jerrod—is among the brightest success stories that have come out of Paul's experience as a culinary educator and mentor. Like Paul, Jerrod was not particularly enthused over conventional education and was in danger of not making it through high school. But just as the young Finkelstein discovered an interest in science by cooking a chicken in the school courtyard, and an older Paul found his burning passion for learning once he enrolled in chef school, Jerrod started coming to school ready to learn every day once he started taking culinary arts in Paul's class. Jerrod graduated and has moved on to a career in the restaurant world, and a letter that his mother wrote expressing her appreciation for Paul's role in her son's life helped convince Prime Minister Stephen Harper that he was deserving of the prestigious Prime Minister's Award for Teaching Excellence in 2012. When Fink went up to receive his award, the PM semi-joked, "I didn't even know we taught culinary arts in Canadian high schools!"

Although the television show is now into reruns, Fink has not stopped in his amazing work with young people from Stratford and across the country. The Edible Schoolyard has evolved into a year-round enterprise, with a local farmer partnering to grow food for the Screaming Avocado in the school's greenhouse. Screaming Avocado students were included among the kitchen team at Rideau Hall in Ottawa when Prince William and his new bride, Kate Middleton, visited Canada for the very first time. Fink and his students recently returned from a third trip to Nunavut, where they've experienced caribou hunting on the Arctic tundra with Inuit elders, as well as healthy eating and exercise programs alongside fellow high schoolers living in the Far North. Their experience working with unique traditional ingredients on their trips to Nunavut led to an extraordinary pop-up fine dining meal in Toronto as part of the Charlie's Burger "mystery restaurant" phenomenon; they were later invited to re-create this northern-themed menu at the venerable James Beard House in New York City, which would be the pinnacle of any chef's career.

Paul Finkelstein continues to contribute to Stratford's culinary history by providing opportunities for the city's young people to cook for one another while coordinating once-in-a-lifetime food experiences for them to participate in. As Alice Waters did for him, he serves as a model for culinary educators across the country and indeed the world, offering proof that if you empower young people to cook, the potentials are limitless.

Chapter 8

Savouring Stratford

Culinary Festivals

In November 2002, the inaugural Stratford Culinary Festival was launched, celebrating the amazing chefs, producers, restaurants and educators who together created the city's storied food scene. Chaired by Janet Sinclair, co-proprietor of Chez Soleil Cooking School, Stratford's first food festival included dinners, cooking workshops and demonstrations and a Sunday Feast of Flavours pairing local restaurants with Ontario microbreweries. All funds raised over the weekend were in support of a scholarship program at the Stratford Chefs School. The event continued annually for two more years, but slow ticket sales and a soft tourism season in 2004 meant that the festival would not be continued past that year.

Then, in January 2008, a young woman from Stratford named Danielle Brodhagen was on vacation from her job at Foster's Inn. She was travelling through the United Kingdom with her partner, a Welshman she had met while he was acting at the Stratford Shakespeare Festival.

They shared a love of great food, as reflected by their vacation itinerary: driving around the countryside, stopping at farm stands and farmers' markets and taking the opportunity at each mealtime to locate a local pub and enjoy a pint alongside whatever food the region of the day was known for.

Of course, her partner was most enthusiastic about the leg of their journey that brought them through his home country, Wales. He made sure they visited lamb farms nestled in the country's rolling hills, stopped off to enjoy pub lunches of Welsh rarebit and purchased local cheeses that had been produced in Wales for generations. Danielle was impressed by the cultural authenticity of everything she was eating and noticed that there was an actual certification program indicating products and restaurants qualifying as true Welsh cuisine.

Then they visited the community of Abergavenny, a picturesque market town in Monmouthshire, Wales. Danielle was immediately struck by the similarities between this rural village and her own hometown of Stratford, Ontario. Abergavenny celebrated its strong agricultural heritage; for example, the town square featured a prominent market hall. There was also a disproportionate number of highly acclaimed restaurants for such a small community (Abergavenny's population is just over fourteen thousand people). As she continued to explore the village as a culinary tourist, she soon discovered that it was most famous for its annual food festival. Each year, during the mid-September harvest season, the village centre was turned into a giant celebration of all the wonderful cuisine Danielle had been experiencing throughout her trip through Wales.

She learned that the Abergavenny Food Festival was established in 1999 by two local farmers in the wake of the BSE crisis and had grown into an event that saw thirty-five thousand people a year coming to the town to peruse more than two hundred food stalls, view cooking demonstrations and presentations by culinary experts, attend a signature tasting event where the best chefs from across the United Kingdom and Wales offered samples of their very best dishes and revel at the Saturday night "Party at the Castle," where the carnival atmosphere was at its pinnacle.

The whole time she was in Abergavenny, Danielle couldn't stop observing how much it reminded her of Stratford. This naturally led to her wondering, *Why couldn't Stratford host the Canadian equivalent of this marvellous food festival?*

One month later, Danielle met with the director of the Stratford Tourism Alliance and shared her vision of a similar food festival in Stratford. He not only thought it was a great idea, but he also hired her to make it happen. Soon Danielle had left her job at Fosters to commit herself fully to making her dream of a large-scale food festival in Stratford happen in September of that same year.

It took a lot of hard work, long hours and relationship building to get the Savour Stratford Perth County Culinary Festival up and running for its first year. But when the weekend in September arrived, a food festival rivalling the Abergavenny spectacle was in place. Fortuitously, the first festival coincided with the twenty-fifth anniversary of the Stratford Chefs School, and this brought back alumni chefs from around the country as both attendees and cooks. There was a farmers' market all along the river with stalls absolutely overflowing with vegetables, honey, fruits and artisan products all produced in the Stratford vicinity; an education tent where some of Canada's best food writers and personalities delivered informative talks; a kids tent where young food lovers could have fun all weekend with hands-on activities and entertainment; nonstop music at the band shell on Veterans Drive, featuring local acts; and an event showcasing the area's finest ingredients cooked up by the talented chefs from all the great restaurants in town—the Sunday Tasting Tent.

All the notable people in Stratford came out on that first gorgeous fall Sunday for the Tasting Tent, including the mayor and high-profile actors from the Stratford Shakespeare Festival. Danielle's attention to detail paid off, as everyone in attendance experienced a truly magical afternoon. Live jazz played as patrons sampled incredible food from thirty stations being attended by both the chef *and* the farmer or artisan whose products were featured in the dish. There were five Ontario wineries and five Ontario craft breweries serving the best in local wine and beer to the appreciative guests, as well as desserts, chocolates, coffee and tea from Stratford's confectioners and cafés.

Just nine months after Danielle Brodhagen had come up with the idea of having a food festival in Stratford, the inaugural Savour Stratford Perth County Food Festival was declared a complete success. Five thousand people attended that first year, many of whom were local residents who gained a strong sense of pride in their food-loving community.

Danielle was intent on making it even better the following year. She went to the community and asked for feedback: people felt that it could be more inclusive, since not everyone could afford the pricey ticket for the Tasting Tent. So, in 2009, the Savour Stratford festival added BBQ, Blues and Brews—a Saturday night party where folks could drink cold beer, eat great local barbecued pork and dance to the sounds of a popular blues band. The event was designed to be highly accessible and an opportunity for the people of the local community to really enjoy themselves in the spirit of the festival, and it worked: tickets sold out faster than the Tasting Tent, and everyone agreed that the music, food and energy was the highlight of that year's festival.

Total attendance at the 2009 festival doubled to ten thousand, and everything else increased in size proportionately: the kids tent got bigger and had more programs; the music went later and featured more acts, many of whom had approached the organizers requesting to play just to get the exposure; the farmers' market had even more stalls; and the Tasting Tent expanded to accommodate virtually every restaurant in town and their partner producers. The perception of the festival that second year changed from a local celebration of all things food to a true culinary tourism event, with people travelling to Stratford just to attend. Stratford officially had itself another high-profile festival.

In 2010, the festival continued to grow and evolve. Paul Finkelstein led an open-air group family cook-along at the band shell to kick off the Saturday morning. BBQ, Blues and Brews was a full-blown pig roast, with whole hogs being cooked on a spit on site. The Tasting Tent was now two tents full of amazing cuisine, with swarms of food bloggers and media in attendance—word had definitely got out that this was now Ontario's premier food event. This was confirmed as the 2010 Savour Stratford Festival was honoured with the Best Culinary Tourism Experience Award by the Ontario Culinary Tourism Alliance.

At this point, Danielle and the other Savour Stratford organizers might have decided to rest on their laurels for the 2011 festival, but instead they took it up another notch by bringing in high-profile celebrity chef Chuck Hughes, the Montreal kitchen prodigy and *Iron Chef America* champion who was well known and loved for his Food Network Canada show *Chuck's Day Off*, which had spun off his acclaimed Montreal restaurant Garde-Manger. *Top Chef Canada* finalist Connie Desousa also brought some star power to the event, hosting a "Women in Food" brunch on the Sunday morning. The festival expanded that year to also include a cooking demonstration stage in Market Square, and Danielle's dream of taking over the entire city with a food festival—just like they did in Abergavenny—was realized. And once again, Danielle and her team were honoured, this time with OCTA's Culinary Tourism Leadership Award.

The following year was slightly disappointing, with poor weather putting a damper on attendance and outdoor programs. But Food Network Canada star David Rocco was a bright light that shone through the rain. The 2012 festival theme was "Our Culinary Heritage," and many of the stories and themes of this book—including the agricultural traditions, the stories of Stratford's great restaurants and the legacy of the Stratford Chefs School—were all held up for celebration.

The 2013 festival was again a disappointment due to inclement weather, with an entire roster of Friday night programs literally

Chuck Hughes, Montreal chef, winner of *Iron Chef America* and host of Food Network Canada's *Chuck's Day Off*, does a cooking demonstration at the 2012 Savour Stratford Perth County Culinary Festival. *Stratford Tourism Alliance.*

washed out by torrential rainstorms. However, the festival theme was "International Goes Local," and the chef ambassador who was called on to oversee the festivities was none other than Vikram Vij, the highly successful Vancouver restaurateur famous for bringing together the flavours of India with those of other cultures in creative fusion dishes. Fortunately for those who avoided the event due to the terrible weather, a live streaming Internet broadcast of Vij's Saturday workshop at The Local Community Food Centre was available for anyone in the world to enjoy. And on the culinary stage, Roger Mooking, another Food Network Canada Star, delivered a spice-filled demonstration.

The 2014 Savour Stratford festival theme is "Coast to Coast to Coast," in celebration of Canadian cuisine from all provinces and territories. The celebrity chefs will include *Top Chef Canada* winners Dale Mackay and Carl Heinrich, along with other *Top Chef Canada* contenders: Newfoundland chef Todd Perrin and Chef Rich Francis, who specializes in cuisine from his Northern Aboriginal culture. They will join Montreal chef Derek Dammann; Whistler, British Columbia chef James Walt; Alberta's Paul

Roger Mooking from Food Network Canada's *Everyday Exotic* heating up the stage with bold spices at the 2013 Savour Stratford Perth County Culinary Festival. *Stratford Tourism Alliance.*

Rogalski; and vegan chef Doug McNish. This year's festival corresponds with the thirtieth anniversary of the culmination of the Stratford Chefs School's first season, so there will be a special spirit of celebration in the air. For the first time ever, the Savour Stratford Festival will be held in July—when the chance for the kind of wet, cold weather than has put a damper on several of the recent festivals will be greatly reduced.

But today, the activities of Savour Stratford are not restricted to the three-day festival. The culinary tourism arm of the Stratford Tourism Alliance coordinates seasonal food experiences for people visiting the city. This includes the popular Bacon and Ale Trail, where people who love beer and bacon (and who doesn't!?) are able to follow a self-guided route through bars, restaurants and stores, with an offering at each stop. Mercer Hall offers a bacon-rimmed Caesar cocktail; the little boutique SmallMart gives participants bacon-flavoured soap; and Molly Bloom's pub serves its bacon-heavy Loaded Baked Potato Soup along with a pint of craft beer. Similarly, the Savour Stratford Christmas Trail invites people to visit multiple sites, where they are offered Yuletide food treats, including a giant candy cane at Chocolate Barr's. That site also features prominently on the Chocolate Trail run by Savour Stratford; local confectioners, including the legendary Rheo Thompson's Candies, are found along the route, as is fudge from the Rocky Mountain Chocolate Factory.

In addition, Savour Stratford coordinates some important annual events and networking opportunities through which producers, restaurants and other members of the food community are able to connect with one another. The Perth County Food Summit has been running since 2010 and provides a platform for stakeholders in the food landscape to discuss issues, such as the disappearance of local abattoirs for farmers to have their meat processed, and to communicate ideas. In June 2012, Canadian food laureate Anita Stewart came to Stratford, where she participated in a panel discussing "What is Canadian Cuisine?" Fellow panelists included culinary arts educator Paul Finkelstein, Chef Jeff Crump from the Ancaster Mill and Monforte Dairy cheese heir Daniel Szoller. Although the consensus was that Canadian cuisine was an elusive concept to pin down, the passionate discussion that was facilitated by the Savour Stratford organization demonstrated how the city of Stratford celebrates and epitomizes our national culinary heritage. Savour Stratford also collected a database of local food producers and created an application for its website whereby people seeking out local food ingredients can search by farm or by product to find out where to get it in Perth County.

There is another food festival in Stratford that has also taken place in September, and since its inception in 2007, it has been focused on celebrating one storied, pungent ingredient: garlic! The old Stratford Fairgrounds hosts the annual Stratford Garlic Festival, an homage to the "stinking rose," which was founded by August's Harvest garlic farmer Warren Ham from nearby Gadshill and has been run by the Kiwanis Club every year. The more than sixty vendors who attend the event offer every type of garlic product one could imagine (and then some!): garlic fudge, garlic ice cream, garlic tempura, garlic shooters, garlic peanut brittle, garlic buttertarts, garlic pickled eggs and many more. There is seed garlic for sale, garlic cooking demos, garlic braiding sessions, garlic cook-offs and hats that look like garlic cloves. If it's got anything to do with garlic, it is at the Stratford Garlic Festival, which in 2014 will happen on September 6–7. Hint: Bring a mint!

There are also two popular events each winter that bring food lovers out in droves no matter how bad the weather is. Soups On! is a fundraiser for the Alzheimer's Society during which community groups, restaurants and businesses all vie to outdo one another by making the best soup. Thousands pack the Rotary Complex to try dozens of soup creations, with plaques awarded to the best offerings, including the coveted "People's Choice." Heartburn Day is a similar format where companies, restaurants and groups like churches come together to raise money for the Heart and Stroke Society by making their best chili recipes. Both events raise tens of thousands of dollars for their charities and demonstrate that the best way to get people in Stratford out for a good cause is to build an event around lots of good food!

There is a lot to celebrate in Stratford around food, and the events that have taken place there reflect a strong spirit of culinary revelry. The idea that there is one festival in Stratford—the Shakespeare Festival—is one that has been challenged by the emergence of these amazing food fests. Today, Stratford is not just a place that celebrates its own culinary heritage and culture. It also celebrates the wonderful food that is found across the country and around the world!

Chapter 9

Food Security

From Stigma to Empowerment

Stratford's food history reflects a community that has enjoyed ever-increasing abundance in terms of its productive agricultural heritage, its prolific restaurant and retail sector and its leading-edge culinary education programs. But there is another important area of the city's edible history that could be easily neglected but which deserves attention. It has evolved remarkably from a topic that was once unspoken due to stigma to a movement that Stratford is currently leading the way on nationally: food security.

Some have incorrectly assumed that a community that's become famous for feeding itself and its visitors would have no citizens living without access to good food. Indeed, that false premise proved deadly back in 1856. That year, an Italian carver named Texter arrived in Stratford with his family. Although a talented craftsperson in stone and wood, there was virtually no demand for his artistry, leaving him without enough income to adequately feed his family. But he was too ashamed and proud to admit it and ask for help. Tragically, a baby died. Then an older child. It was only then that people realized their own neighbours were starving in their midst. John Scott, the grocer, ran to his shop and filled a basket with food that was then taken over to the Texter home by his wife. Upon seeing the food at her door, Mrs. Texter broke down, "If you had come sooner, my children might be alive. You are too late!" Mrs. Scott, horrified that people—children!—were dying of hunger in her village, cried out, "Why did you not tell us?"

The wooden Indian that was the namesake for the early "Indian Block" was created by a man named Texter, who was unable to feed his family because no one would purchase his carvings. *Stratford-Perth Archives.*

Mr. and Mrs. Scott admirably recognized that the stigma and shame regarding asking neighbours for handouts had resulted in the death of the two Texter children. They responded in a way that supported the family while also promoting their dignity: they bought an ornate statue of a life-size Indian that had been masterfully carved by Texter using a log that had originally been cut when the city was clearing land for the Market Building site. This fine wooden figure was a fixture outside the Scotts' grocery store on Market Street for many years, and this led to the stretch of stores along that road being historically referred to as the "Indian Block."

This was the beginning of a unique historical storyline that has seen Stratford residents support one another's food needs in ways that transcend mere charitable handouts.

World War I was a period during which communities across the western world, including Stratford, faced the dual crises of shortages and high food prices. In an era when everyone did what they could at home to support the war effort abroad, the Stratford Horticultural Society created a Vacant Lot Cultivation Committee. Areas that were once sitting as brownfields were transformed by brigades of gardeners into community vegetable patches overflowing with squash and beans. Any tract of land that was not being used was appropriated as a resource for food production: property sitting idle, undeveloped subdivisions, private land that was not being utilized, two acres of parkland along the Avon River and ten empty building lots in the Avon Ward were turned over to food production by average citizens willing to do whatever they could to feed their community.

All the schools also created their own educational war gardens, and just as they might have competed with one another in spelling bees and baseball, so, too, did they show their school pride in rivalries for cultivating the most productive school gardens. In fact, a trophy was awarded by Dr. D.H. Eidt to the Stratford school with the best school garden, which Hamlet Public School won in triumph! The competitive approach to increasing the food supply was extended out to the greater community, as the Stratford Horticultural Society expanded its annual Flower Show to also include a Vacant Lot Vegetable Show in 1918.

By the end of the war, there were, remarkably, 450 community vegetable plots being tended to in the city of Stratford. In an era marked by war, strife, loss and scarcity, fresh vegetables provided rare opportunities for joy, pride and health for its citizens. The last summer of the war saw a bumper crop in the community's war gardens. To handle all the produce and ensure that the season's bounty could be utilized throughout the year, the North Perth Community Canning Centre was created on Erie Street, processing seven tonnes of produce in six weeks. Canning equipment had been supplied by the government of Ontario; the Canadian Red Cross supplied vinegar, sugar, spices and containers. The area's Women's Institutes and the Stratford Imperial Order of the Daughters of the Empire, as well as other community service groups, all pitched in on the six-week mother of all community canning sessions.

When the war was over, a new group of vulnerable citizens returned from the front in the form of injured soldiers. Fifty-five war gardens continued to be maintained by the Stratford Horticultural Society to provide food for these returning fighters who had been crippled.

During World War II, the Stratford Horticultural Society joined other Ontario horticultural societies to send seeds, fertilizer and growing instructions to people living in war-torn countries in Europe, as well as prisoners of war. The conditions of scarcity and deprivation were intense, with food highly controlled and rationed. For those experiencing these conditions of near-starvation, the opportunity to grow and eat fresh produce was invaluable.

In 1945, the president of the Stratford Horticultural Society encouraged everyone to help win the war by planting what was now called a "Victory Garden":

> *We are reminded of the need for increase in food production, because in addition to meeting the needs of the Armed Forces and our Allies, the liberated countries are looking to us for food. Every additional pound of vegetables grown in our home gardens, and used by ourselves and perhaps some of our friends who cannot work a garden, can therefore mean that much of the farmers' production is available for distribution to the larger centres in our own country, to the Armed Forces, our Allies and the liberated countries. No very great gardening skill is needed to grow most vegetables and fortunately seeds are cheap enough. Experience gained should result in the production of bigger and better crops. Then, too, the home-garden growing of at least some vegetables pays. It pays anyone who is physically able and has or can make a little spare time. It pays in better health derived from working with the "good soil." One doesn't need to go in for such activity over strenuously; it pays in the satisfaction of obtaining really fresh vegetables of your own growing for*

your own table. To those who have not done so, we earnestly recommend that you plan and plant a Victory Garden and note the benefits.

Gardening was recognized as a noble contribution to the war effort as home production took domestic pressure off the food supply so it could be exported to areas devastated by conflict. The payoff was not just great food but also improved health and a sense of satisfaction among those who took up this challenge.

Another era characterized by food insecurity across North America, including Stratford, was the Great Depression of the 1930s. Although Stratford had become a centre for jobs related to industrial manufacturing and railway activity, in the Dirty Thirties, those who had previously enjoyed stable employment and professions were found knocking door to door looking for odd jobs. Bread lines appeared. Even those with jobs were finding it difficult to keep their families fed as the economy started to collapse. People were laid off, and those with salaries were getting their wages cut, sometimes willingly so that fellow employees could keep their jobs.

The small corner grocery store was an important source of food for Stratford households. During the 1930s, many owners of these stores provided temporary food relief for households that were struggling. For example, Ed Doadt was a grocer whose store was located at the corner of Downie and Bridges Streets; he offered his customers accounts so they could settle up on payday. But even if some were experiencing unemployment, he would let them run up tabs to feed their families, and he would let these accounts go unpaid for months. However, by the end of the Depression, almost all the credit he had provided to families in Stratford was eventually paid back. These grocers appreciated that the community supported them and their businesses, so when they had the opportunity to support those loyal customers who had lost their ability to put bread on the table for their families due to wage cuts or layoffs, they did not hesitate.

Other local organizations also helped with food relief during the Depression. The Salvation Army issued meal tickets to those who were hungry, many of whom were transients. At that time, Stratford's location as a railway town led to the congregation of homeless "hobos" who rode the rails in a nomadic lifestyle and congregated in "jungles." To help feed these wandering populations, a soup kitchen was opened next to the Kroehler plant, the only official one that was set up during the '30s.

But there was also an unofficial soup kitchen that arose at that time. In the 1930s, petty crimes were rife, but for the most part, the culprits could hardly be labeled "criminals" since they were mostly stealing food to stay alive and clothes for their families. In fact, some stole with the goal of getting caught so they could get sent to the Stratford Jail, where they would at least have a roof over their head for the night and three square meals a day. Each night, the jail would be crowded with hungry transients who had willfully ended up in the clink with the hope of enjoying a bowl of the prison's famous soup, which was prepared using bones and leftovers donated by local restaurants. The police chief at the time later recalled, "Every night we boiled up a big pot of soup and, before releasing our 'tenants' in the morning, they got a big bowl of the night's boil. We canvassed city restaurants for bones and leftovers and tossed them all in the pot. It was mighty good soup!"

At times, community gardens were themselves the sites of desperate thievery. People on welfare or relief during the Depression were given plots of land to garden behind Avondale Cemetery. These tucked-away gardens were often raided by hungry, unemployed people for fresh vegetables. They knew that the worst thing that could happen if they got caught was to go to the jail—where they could enjoy a hot bowl of its famous soup.

In more recent times, Stratford residents have continued to grow food for themselves through community gardens. There is a community garden on Franklin Avenue that members of the Stratford Horticulture Society have been cultivating for several years along with other green thumbs. In 2010, McCully's Hill Farm, located just outside Stratford near St. Marys, decided that growing vegetables for its farm store would be a lot easier if it collaborated with people who had no land but wanted to grow food for themselves, and the McCully's Hill Farm Community Garden Co-op was formed. In 2010, two friends—one with a backyard but no time or energy for gardening, and another with no land but a strong desire to grow food—partnered to create the Stratford Urban Farming Experiment, which sought to link others with available lawn space to people who would be willing to create and tend to a veggie garden plot. On a vacant city property near the train station, a faith-driven man has spent several summers tending to "God's Green Acre," a small urban farm where he grows food with the sole intention to donate to the food banks. And for the last few years, a law office at the corner of Waterloo and Cobourg Streets has planted a few raised beds with a sign indicating that the food grown there was free for the taking for anyone who wanted it.

The economic downturn of the 1980s in Canada saw the emergence of a new phenomenon for providing what was originally supposed to be temporary emergency food relief for those who suddenly found themselves unable to feed their families: the food bank. The Stratford House of Blessing was founded by Florence Kehl in the 1980s as a faith-driven resource for helping those in the community experiencing times of hardship and need. By 2009, the year Mrs. Kehl retired and handed over the management of her charity to an executive director, it was the busiest of six food banks located in Stratford, providing monthly food relief to hundreds of individuals and families each year. Unfortunately, the conditions that arose in the 1980s were hardly improved on over the thirty years that followed, and food banks became permanent fixtures responding to ongoing food insecurity in communities such as Stratford.

In 2009, a recent graduate of the Stratford Chefs School who was working as a sous chef at the Old Prune and also as a Chefs School instructor had an idea to promote food security in Stratford by putting to use some of the leftover ingredients that were often thrown out at the school at the end of the week. It disturbed him that quality food was being wasted while people in his community were struggling to put food on the table. He rallied students at the school to join him on their day off and cook two hundred portions of soup each week, which were then vacuum-packaged and donated to the House of Blessing, where he was a regular volunteer. The initiative, called Stone Soup, also inspired local growers and other restaurant kitchens to donate items for the weekly soup sessions.

In addition to the food banks, the Stratford community also responded to the problem of food insecurity by providing community meals, most of which were provided in churches such as Knox Presbyterian Church. By 2010, there was a hot meal available almost every night of the week during the winter months. Unfortunately, due to the challenges of coordinating volunteers during the summer months, there were very few community meals on offer between May and October.

But among those who were running food banks or volunteering on community meals, a paradox was becoming evident: in the city of Stratford—which was becoming known far and wide for its great food, largely due to its location in the heart of a prime agricultural region—some people were still unable to access healthy, local food.

This problem was challenged through the formation in 2008 of the Perth County Food Security Coalition, which was convened by the United Way of Perth-Huron and the Perth District Health Unit. They invited all the food banks, community meal providers and student nutrition program coordinators, as well as representatives from shelters and social service providers working with the low-income community, to come together and collaborate. They discussed how they could all work together to promote healthier eating among those who were being excluded from Stratford's bountiful food supply. They came up with an innovative idea: create a centralized warehouse where large-scale donations of surplus food from agriculture, processors, retailers and producers could be taken in and distributed out to all the not-for-profit organizations working to connect people with good food.

Then, as the coalition was getting prepared to take that vision and make it a reality, an opportunity arose to expand it into something truly extraordinary. In Toronto, an organization called The Stop Community Food Centre was rewriting the book on food security programs in Canada. Since its humble beginnings as a food bank in a low-income apartment high-rise, The Stop had evolved into a place where people came to enjoy meals together; participate in cooking classes; work alongside one another in community gardens; access healthy, fresh food through its revamped food pantry; and advocate for a more socially just community through anti-poverty activism campaigns. Food-insecure community members were no longer passive recipients of food charities but rather had become empowered cooks, gardeners and activists in their west end neighbourhood. Over its thirty-year history, The Stop had evolved into what was recognized as the gold standard for community food programs, which included its expansion into the Wychwood Barns, a former streetcar repair garage that was transformed into a community food centre, complete with a greenhouse, a community kitchen, an outdoor bake oven and even a weekly farmers' market. When UK celebrity chef Jamie Oliver visited The Stop in 2010, he turned to its then executive director Nick Saul and told him that he'd been all around the world visiting food projects but had never seen anything as wonderful as The Stop. As he stood in the greenhouse, he held his hands up and exclaimed, "There should be one of these in every city!"

Nick Saul couldn't agree with him more. In fact, he was in the process of initiating a national network of community food centres across the

The author harvesting onions with a young urban farmer in the community gardens at The Local Community Food Centre. *The Local Community Food Centre.*

country. And the site for the first community food centre he planned to create outside of The Stop? Stratford, of course!

Saul's new organization, Community Food Centres Canada, partnered with the United Way of Perth-Huron to renovate the former Stratford Farmers Co-op on Erie Street and turn it into The Local Community Food Centre, which opened its doors in November 2012. The building had everything the project needed: a warehouse space to accommodate the food distribution centre originally envisioned by the Perth County Food Security Coalition; a retail space that was renovated to include an expansive community kitchen, as well as a comfortable dining room for community meals; and even a 2,500-square-foot greenhouse that would allow for community gardening activities to take place year-round.

Today "The Local" is a thriving community hub where the great food Stratford has become famous for is available to all regardless of their social or economic status. The distribution centre is called the Storehouse and focuses its efforts on taking in donations and strategic purchases of fresh, healthy, local food on behalf of the area's food banks, student nutrition programs, shelters, group homes and community meals. The community kitchen hosts daily food skills programs during which people are taught how to make healthy meals for their families on a budget. Community meals take place three times a week in the form of a Monday night dinner, a seniors lunch on Wednesdays and a breakfast on Thursdays that begins with a free yoga class for anyone who is interested. The communal gardens and greenhouse give everyone the opportunity to help grow food for the meals and programs, as well as to bring some home for themselves. And activism and advocacy initiatives empower Stratford's low-income community to fight for a society where food banks will one day be unnecessary because people will have what they need to feed themselves.

Remember that Stratford Chefs School instructor who started the Stone Soup initiative to provide high-quality soups to the food bank? His name is Jordan Lassaline, and he is now the chef-educator at The Local, where it is his job every day to ensure that everyone in the Stratford community benefits from the wonderful food for which the city is known.

The history of the issue of food security in Stratford has therefore evolved in a remarkable way, from a situation where children were dying because of the shame and stigma of living in hunger to a community where the vision of a place where everyone can eat well is coming closer to being realized than perhaps ever before.

Conclusion

When one drives into Stratford, the welcome sign says it all: "Stratford: Home of the Stratford Shakespeare Festival, and the Ontario Pork Congress."

Even with the presence of one of the finest theatre festivals in North America, food still occupies a space that is front and centre. The mix produced through the mingling of a rich agricultural heritage with a modern arts mecca has resulted in something truly unique: a community of just over thirty thousand residents that boasts some of the best restaurants in the country, some cutting-edge culinary education programs and a model for a sustainable food system that provides access to local food not just for those who are rich, but for everyone. No wonder the culinary festival that takes place in the city each year is so popular: there's a lot to celebrate!

Bibliography

Anita Stewart's Food Day Canada. "The Church Restaurant and the Belfry, Stratford, Ontario." http://fooddaycanada.ca/events/the-church-restaurant-the-belfry-stratford-ontario.

———. "The Old Prune, Stratford, Ontario." http://fooddaycanada.ca/events/the-old-prune-stratford-ontario.

Bain, Richard, and Christopher Plummer. *Stratford*. Erin, ON: Boston Mills Press, 1998.

Barer-Stein, Thelma. *You Eat What You Are: People, Culture and Food Traditions*. Toronto: Firefly Books, 1999.

Bart-Riedstra, Carolyn. *Stratford: Images of Canada*. St. Catharines, ON: Arcadia, 2002.

———. *Stratford: Its Heritage and Its Festival*. Toronto: J. Lorimer, 1999.

Bietz, Mike. "Stratford Chefs School Blows Out Candles on 30 Years." *Stratford Beacon Herald*, October 24, 2003.

Charpryk, Jim. "Stratford to Host Conference on Canadian Cuisine." *Stratford Beacon Herald*, February 4, 1993.

Chilton, Susan. "Stratford Chefs School Graduates Can Dish It Out." *The Record*, January 25, 2001.

Cluff, Paul. "Culinary Festival to Showcase Chefs, Schools, Restaurants." *Stratford Beacon Herald*, October 26, 2002.

———. "Soup-er Idea Benefits Local Food Banks." *Stratford Beacon Herald*, February 23, 2009.

Coates, Rosemary. "High Standards, Attention to Detail Set Stratford Chefs School Apart." *Stratford Beacon Herald*, December 21, 1995.

Coleman, Thelma. *The Canada Company*. Stratford, ON: County of Perth & Cumming Publishers, 1978.

———. "History of the Canada Company (Covering in Particular the Huron Tract)." Unpublished. Perth County Historical Board, Stratford, Ontario, 1975.

———. *Stratford, the City Beautiful: The Story of the Stratford and District Horticultural Society, 1878–1978*. Stratford, ON: Canadian Household Advertising Ltd., 1978.

Denney, Frances L. "Transforming Cooks Into Chefs." *The Record*, October 17, 1984.

Ferris, Neal. *The Archaeology of Native-Lived Colonialism: Challenging History in the Great Lakes*. Tuscon: University of Arizona Press, 2009.

Food Service and Hospitality. "Eleanor Kane Retires from Stratford Chefs School." http://www.foodserviceandhospitality.com/central/ontario-news/5091-eleanor-kane-retires-from-stratford-chefs-school.html.

Genes Restaurant. "The History." http://www.genesrestaurant.ca/genes_history.htm.

The Gentle Rain Natural Health Food Store. "About Us." http://www.thegentlerain.ca/page.php?id=2&name=about_us.php.

Guelph Mercury. "Stratford Chefs School Chooses Journalist Ian Brown as Its Writer-in-Residence." http://www.guelphmercury.com/news-story/2709703-stratford-chefs-school-chooses-journalist-ian-brown-as-its-writer-in-residence.

Hornbeck Tanner, Helen. *Atlas of Great Lakes Indian History*. Norman: University of Oklahoma Press, 1987.

Hughes, Pat. "Farmers Encouraged to Work Together to Ensure Future of Ontario Agriculture." *Stratford Beacon Herald*, September 23, 1993.

Johnston, Walter Stafford. *History of Perth County to 1967*. Stratford, ON: County of Perth, 1967.

Kingsmill, David. "Chefs School in Spotlight at Stratford." *Toronto Star*, April 10. 1985.

Kroes, Lindsay. *Gather by the Avon*. New Hamburg, ON: Recollections Publications, 2013.

Leitch, Adelaide. *Floodtides of Fortune: The Story of Stratford and the Progress of the City through Two Centuries*. Stratford, ON: Corporation of the City of Stratford, 1980.

Lennon, M.J. *A Stratford Album: Memories of the Festival City*. Erin, ON: Boston Mills Press, 1985.

Madelyn's Diner. "About Us." http://www.madelynsdiner.ca/services.asp.

Monckton, Stephen G. "Plants and the Archaeology of the Invisible." *Before Ontario: The Archaeology of a Province.* Edited by Marit K. Munson and Susan M. Jamieson. Montreal: McGill University Press, 2013.

Nanaimo Daily News. "International Chefs Broaden Horizons of Students at Stratford Chefs School." http://www.nanaimodailynews.com/life/international-chefs-broaden-horizons-of-students-at-stratford-chefs-school-1.795653.

Needs-Howarth, Susan. "Animals and Archaeologists." *Before Ontario: The Archaeology of a Province.* Edited by Marit K. Munson and Susan M. Jamieson. Montreal: McGill University Press, 2013.

Nuttal Smith, Chris. "Blogger Dishes on the Art of French Baking." *Globe and Mail,* November 8, 2011. http://www.theglobeandmail.com/life/food-and-wine/food-trends/blogger-dishes-on-the-art-of-french-baking/article4183129.

O'Connor, Donal. "Chefs School Hosting First National Food Conference." *Stratford Beacon Herald,* September 16, 1993.

Perth Pork Products. "The deMartines Family Farm." http://www.perthporkproducts.com/view.php?public/Our_Farm.

Pettigrew, John. *Stratford: The First Thirty Years.* Toronto: MacMillan of Canada, 1985.

Riedstra, Lutzen. *History of Perth County 1867 to 2003.* Stratford, ON: Corporation of the County of Perth, 2003.

Robinson, Dean. *Reflections: A History of the Stratford Agricultural Society, 1841–1991.* Stratford, ON: Stratford Agricultural Society, 1991.

Schmalz, Peter S. *The Ojibwa of Southern Ontario.* Toronto: University of Toronto Press, 1991.

Sewell, Dianne. "Chefs Urged to Keep Up with Shifting Tastes." *Stratford Beacon Herald,* June 21, 1993.

Shypula, Brian. "Chefs School Focus of New TV Series." *Stratford Beacon Herald,* December 26, 2007.

———. "Growing Stratford Chefs School Has Bigger Quarters, More Staff." *Stratford Beacon Herald,* October 23, 1991.

———. "A Lip-Smacking Event." *Stratford Beacon Herald,* November 8, 2004.

———. "Stratford Chefs School Show Cooks Up a Gemini Award." *Stratford Beacon Herald,* October 23, 2006.

Stacey, Steve. The Local-Come-Lately. http://local-come-lately.blogspot.ca.

Stafford, Ellen. *Stratford: Around and About.* Stratford, ON: Fanfare Books, 1972.

Stelmach, Bo. "January at the School." Stratford Chefs School Blog. http://stratfordchef.wordpress.com.

Stratford Chefs School. "Founding Directors." http://www.stratfordchef. com/founding-directors.

———. "Joseph Hoare Gastronomic Writer in Residence Program." https://stratfordchef.com/Portals/0/GWIR_CaseStatement_D10.pdf.

Stratford Gazette. "Big Names on Roster for Culinary Festival." September 5, 2008.

Stratford Tourism. "Historic Downtown Walk." http://www.visitstratford. ca/media/pdf/historic-walk.pdf.

Strauss, Bob. "Woolly Mammoth." About.com—Dinosaurs. http:// dinosaurs.about.com/od/mesozoicmammals/p/mammuthus.htm.

Turnbull, Larke. "Chefs School Heats Up Restaurant Scene." *Stratford Beacon Herald*, May 27, 2000.

Westley, Meg. "Culinary Stratford Stories." http://megwestley.wordpress. com/culinary-stratford-stories.

Weston, Linda. "City's Uniqueness Part of Program to Train Top Chefs." *Stratford Beacon Herald*, January 12, 1984.

———. "The Making of a Chef, Not a Cook." *Stratford Beacon Herald*, January 13, 1984.

Your Local Market Co-operative. "About." http://www.yourlocalmarketcoop. com/about.html.

Index

About the Author

There is a bit of an undercurrent that lies beneath some of the more recent stories included in this edible history of Stratford: the author's involvement.

I moved to Stratford, my wife Lisa's hometown, in 2009. The story about the day we decided to move here reveals my motivation to live in a city where food is at the heart of so much that happens in the community. It was a Sunday in September, and I was in the small Eastern Ontario village of Batawa, a former factory town that had seen better days. I had spent the summer spearheading a local food project there that was part of a larger community rejuvenation initiative. Unfortunately, food wasn't an important element in the town's social fabric, and despite my best efforts, the only people I could get excited about cooking, gardening and local agriculture were the town's school kids.

I was sitting by myself in an empty restaurant where I'd hosted an all-local, community garden–fresh brunch throughout the summer. I guess word didn't get out that we were also serving into the fall. Bored silly, I called my wife, who was three hours away visiting her parents in Stratford. She couldn't really hear me over the music. Outdoor techno on a Sunday afternoon!? Hmm. She was attending the Savour Stratford Perth County Culinary Festival.

It was too bad that I wasn't there with her, she yelled over the music. I would have loved it—a farmers' market, cooking demonstrations, chef tastings, jazz, breakbeats, street performers and more. A food carnival!

The silence on my end was deafening. I recall a vision of tumbleweeds rolling through the vacant, cavernous hall where I sat, the sole patron of my own food event. Definitely not a carnival. I asked my wife how she'd feel about moving back home. And three months later, we lived here.

From the moment I got to Stratford, my goal was to participate in any food-related event or initiative I could find. I met Danielle Brodhagen, the founder of Savour Stratford, and she invited me to join Slow Food Perth County. Through that organization, I met Paul Finkelstein, and the next spring, he hired me as his assistant at the Screaming Avocado Café, where I worked for the semester. Together with Paul and his students, we put nine school gardens in the elementary schools of Stratford. I was also extremely fortunate to join him and his class on a culinary trip to Cambridge Bay, Nunavut, and was able to write about our adventures—which included catching caribou on the Arctic tundra with the Inuit elders—in an article I published in *Canadian Living* magazine.

I collaborated with the nearby McCully's Hill Farm to establish a new community garden there. I volunteered with the new Slow Food Sunday Market and became the market coordinator, which lasted for four years. I worked on the 2010–13 Savour Stratford Perth County Culinary Festival committees. I volunteered on one of the community meals in town.

I was also hired by the Stratford Tourism Alliance to be the city's first-ever official food blogger, the Local Come Lately. My blog posts narrated my experience as a food lovin' newcomer in a food lovin' town, getting to know all the local farmers, restaurants, activists and culinary characters who make the Stratford scene so vibrant and interesting.

Then, in 2011, my passion for food and community was rewarded with an unparalleled opportunity when I was hired as the executive director of The Local Community Food Centre. Through my work at "The Local," I've been able to bring together all my interests—cooking, gardening, community building, education, local food and sustainable agriculture—and contribute them towards making Stratford an even better place for people to live. Through the power of food, I have been able to help break down barriers, empower people who were formerly isolated and marginalized, promote health and mobilize activism efforts towards a fairer food system and a more equitable Canadian society.

Moving to Stratford was the best decision I ever made. I can't think of anywhere else where a person whose sole motivation is to build community through food could experience what I've seen happen here in just five years.